Scepticism: A Very Short Introduction

VERY SHORT INTRODUCTIONS are for anyone wanting a stimulating and accessible way into a new subject. They are written by experts, and have been translated into more than 45 different languages.

The series began in 1995, and now covers a wide variety of topics in every discipline. The VSI library currently contains over 600 volumes—a Very Short Introduction to everything from Psychology and Philosophy of Science to American History and Relativity—and continues to grow in every subject area.

Very Short Introductions available now:

ABOLITIONISM Richard S. Newman
ACCOUNTING Christopher Nobes
ADAM SMITH Christopher J. Berry
ADOLESCENCE Peter K. Smith
ADVERTISING Winston Fletcher
AFRICAN AMERICAN RELIGION
    Eddie S. Glaude Jr
AFRICAN HISTORY John Parker
    and Richard Rathbone
AFRICAN POLITICS Ian Taylor
AFRICAN RELIGIONS
    Jacob K. Olupona
AGEING Nancy A. Pachana
AGNOSTICISM Robin Le Poidevin
AGRICULTURE Paul Brassley
    and Richard Soffe
ALEXANDER THE GREAT
    Hugh Bowden
ALGEBRA Peter M. Higgins
AMERICAN CULTURAL HISTORY
    Eric Avila
AMERICAN FOREIGN RELATIONS
    Andrew Preston
AMERICAN HISTORY Paul S. Boyer
AMERICAN IMMIGRATION
    David A. Gerber
AMERICAN LEGAL HISTORY
    G. Edward White
AMERICAN NAVAL HISTORY
    Craig L. Symonds
AMERICAN POLITICAL HISTORY
    Donald Critchlow
AMERICAN POLITICAL PARTIES
    AND ELECTIONS L. Sandy Maisel

AMERICAN POLITICS
    Richard M. Valelly
THE AMERICAN PRESIDENCY
    Charles O. Jones
THE AMERICAN REVOLUTION
    Robert J. Allison
AMERICAN SLAVERY
    Heather Andrea Williams
THE AMERICAN WEST Stephen Aron
AMERICAN WOMEN'S HISTORY
    Susan Ware
ANAESTHESIA Aidan O'Donnell
ANALYTIC PHILOSOPHY
    Michael Beaney
ANARCHISM Colin Ward
ANCIENT ASSYRIA Karen Radner
ANCIENT EGYPT Ian Shaw
ANCIENT EGYPTIAN ART AND
    ARCHITECTURE Christina Riggs
ANCIENT GREECE Paul Cartledge
THE ANCIENT NEAR EAST
    Amanda H. Podany
ANCIENT PHILOSOPHY Julia Annas
ANCIENT WARFARE
    Harry Sidebottom
ANGELS David Albert Jones
ANGLICANISM Mark Chapman
THE ANGLO-SAXON AGE John Blair
ANIMAL BEHAVIOUR
    Tristram D. Wyatt
THE ANIMAL KINGDOM
    Peter Holland
ANIMAL RIGHTS David DeGrazia
THE ANTARCTIC Klaus Dodds

ANTHROPOCENE Erle C. Ellis
ANTISEMITISM Steven Beller
ANXIETY Daniel Freeman and
    Jason Freeman
THE APOCRYPHAL GOSPELS
    Paul Foster
APPLIED MATHEMATICS
    Alain Goriely
ARCHAEOLOGY Paul Bahn
ARCHITECTURE Andrew Ballantyne
ARISTOCRACY William Doyle
ARISTOTLE Jonathan Barnes
ART HISTORY Dana Arnold
ART THEORY Cynthia Freeland
ARTIFICIAL INTELLIGENCE
    Margaret A. Boden
ASIAN AMERICAN HISTORY
    Madeline Y. Hsu
ASTROBIOLOGY David C. Catling
ASTROPHYSICS James Binney
ATHEISM Julian Baggini
THE ATMOSPHERE Paul I. Palmer
AUGUSTINE Henry Chadwick
AUSTRALIA Kenneth Morgan
AUTISM Uta Frith
AUTOBIOGRAPHY Laura Marcus
THE AVANT GARDE David Cottington
THE AZTECS David Carrasco
BABYLONIA Trevor Bryce
BACTERIA Sebastian G. B. Amyes
BANKING John Goddard and
    John O. S. Wilson
BARTHES Jonathan Culler
THE BEATS David Sterritt
BEAUTY Roger Scruton
BEHAVIOURAL ECONOMICS
    Michelle Baddeley
BESTSELLERS John Sutherland
THE BIBLE John Riches
BIBLICAL ARCHAEOLOGY
    Eric H. Cline
BIG DATA Dawn E. Holmes
BIOGRAPHY Hermione Lee
BIOMETRICS Michael Fairhurst
BLACK HOLES Katherine Blundell
BLOOD Chris Cooper
THE BLUES Elijah Wald
THE BODY Chris Shilling
THE BOOK OF COMMON
    PRAYER Brian Cummings

THE BOOK OF MORMON
    Terryl Givens
BORDERS Alexander C. Diener
    and Joshua Hagen
THE BRAIN Michael O'Shea
BRANDING Robert Jones
THE BRICS Andrew F. Cooper
THE BRITISH CONSTITUTION
    Martin Loughlin
THE BRITISH EMPIRE Ashley Jackson
BRITISH POLITICS Anthony Wright
BUDDHA Michael Carrithers
BUDDHISM Damien Keown
BUDDHIST ETHICS Damien Keown
BYZANTIUM Peter Sarris
C. S. LEWIS James Como
CALVINISM Jon Balserak
CANCER Nicholas James
CAPITALISM James Fulcher
CATHOLICISM Gerald O'Collins
CAUSATION Stephen Mumford
    and Rani Lill Anjum
THE CELL Terence Allen and
    Graham Cowling
THE CELTS Barry Cunliffe
CHAOS Leonard Smith
CHARLES DICKENS Jenny Hartley
CHEMISTRY Peter Atkins
CHILD PSYCHOLOGY Usha Goswami
CHILDREN'S LITERATURE
    Kimberley Reynolds
CHINESE LITERATURE
    Sabina Knight
CHOICE THEORY Michael Allingham
CHRISTIAN ART Beth Williamson
CHRISTIAN ETHICS D. Stephen Long
CHRISTIANITY Linda Woodhead
CIRCADIAN RHYTHMS
    Russell Foster and Leon Kreitzman
CITIZENSHIP Richard Bellamy
CIVIL ENGINEERING
    David Muir Wood
CLASSICAL LITERATURE William Allan
CLASSICAL MYTHOLOGY
    Helen Morales
CLASSICS Mary Beard and
    John Henderson
CLAUSEWITZ Michael Howard
CLIMATE Mark Maslin
CLIMATE CHANGE Mark Maslin

CLINICAL PSYCHOLOGY
Susan Llewelyn and
Katie Aafjes-van Doorn
COGNITIVE NEUROSCIENCE
Richard Passingham
THE COLD WAR Robert McMahon
COLONIAL AMERICA Alan Taylor
COLONIAL LATIN AMERICAN
LITERATURE Rolena Adorno
COMBINATORICS Robin Wilson
COMEDY Matthew Bevis
COMMUNISM Leslie Holmes
COMPARATIVE LITERATURE
Ben Hutchinson
COMPLEXITY John H. Holland
THE COMPUTER Darrel Ince
COMPUTER SCIENCE
Subrata Dasgupta
CONCENTRATION CAMPS
Dan Stone
CONFUCIANISM Daniel K. Gardner
THE CONQUISTADORS
Matthew Restall and
Felipe Fernández-Armesto
CONSCIENCE Paul Strohm
CONSCIOUSNESS Susan Blackmore
CONTEMPORARY ART
Julian Stallabrass
CONTEMPORARY FICTION
Robert Eaglestone
CONTINENTAL PHILOSOPHY
Simon Critchley
COPERNICUS Owen Gingerich
CORAL REEFS Charles Sheppard
CORPORATE SOCIAL
RESPONSIBILITY Jeremy Moon
CORRUPTION Leslie Holmes
COSMOLOGY Peter Coles
CRIME FICTION Richard Bradford
CRIMINAL JUSTICE Julian V. Roberts
CRIMINOLOGY Tim Newburn
CRITICAL THEORY
Stephen Eric Bronner
THE CRUSADES Christopher Tyerman
CRYPTOGRAPHY Fred Piper and
Sean Murphy
CRYSTALLOGRAPHY A. M. Glazer
THE CULTURAL REVOLUTION
Richard Curt Kraus
DADA AND SURREALISM
David Hopkins

DANTE Peter Hainsworth and
David Robey
DARWIN Jonathan Howard
THE DEAD SEA SCROLLS
Timothy H. Lim
DECADENCE David Weir
DECOLONIZATION Dane Kennedy
DEMOCRACY Bernard Crick
DEMOGRAPHY Sarah Harper
DEPRESSION Jan Scott and
Mary Jane Tacchi
DERRIDA Simon Glendinning
DESCARTES Tom Sorell
DESERTS Nick Middleton
DESIGN John Heskett
DEVELOPMENT Ian Goldin
DEVELOPMENTAL BIOLOGY
Lewis Wolpert
THE DEVIL Darren Oldridge
DIASPORA Kevin Kenny
DICTIONARIES Lynda Mugglestone
DINOSAURS David Norman
DIPLOMACY Joseph M. Siracusa
DOCUMENTARY FILM
Patricia Aufderheide
DREAMING J. Allan Hobson
DRUGS Les Iversen
DRUIDS Barry Cunliffe
DYSLEXIA Margaret J. Snowling
EARLY MUSIC Thomas Forrest Kelly
THE EARTH Martin Redfern
EARTH SYSTEM SCIENCE Tim Lenton
ECONOMICS Partha Dasgupta
EDUCATION Gary Thomas
EGYPTIAN MYTH Geraldine Pinch
EIGHTEENTH-CENTURY BRITAIN
Paul Langford
THE ELEMENTS Philip Ball
EMOTION Dylan Evans
EMPIRE Stephen Howe
ENGELS Terrell Carver
ENGINEERING David Blockley
THE ENGLISH LANGUAGE
Simon Horobin
ENGLISH LITERATURE Jonathan Bate
THE ENLIGHTENMENT
John Robertson
ENTREPRENEURSHIP Paul Westhead
and Mike Wright
ENVIRONMENTAL ECONOMICS
Stephen Smith

ENVIRONMENTAL ETHICS
  Robin Attfield
ENVIRONMENTAL LAW
  Elizabeth Fisher
ENVIRONMENTAL POLITICS
  Andrew Dobson
EPICUREANISM Catherine Wilson
EPIDEMIOLOGY Rodolfo Saracci
ETHICS Simon Blackburn
ETHNOMUSICOLOGY Timothy Rice
THE ETRUSCANS Christopher Smith
EUGENICS Philippa Levine
THE EUROPEAN UNION
  Simon Usherwood and John Pinder
EUROPEAN UNION LAW
  Anthony Arnull
EVOLUTION Brian and
  Deborah Charlesworth
EXISTENTIALISM Thomas Flynn
EXPLORATION Stewart A. Weaver
EXTINCTION Paul B. Wignall
THE EYE Michael Land
FAIRY TALE Marina Warner
FAMILY LAW Jonathan Herring
FASCISM Kevin Passmore
FASHION Rebecca Arnold
FEMINISM Margaret Walters
FILM Michael Wood
FILM MUSIC Kathryn Kalinak
FILM NOIR James Naremore
THE FIRST WORLD WAR
  Michael Howard
FOLK MUSIC Mark Slobin
FOOD John Krebs
FORENSIC PSYCHOLOGY
  David Canter
FORENSIC SCIENCE Jim Fraser
FORESTS Jaboury Ghazoul
FOSSILS Keith Thomson
FOUCAULT Gary Gutting
THE FOUNDING FATHERS
  R. B. Bernstein
FRACTALS Kenneth Falconer
FREE SPEECH Nigel Warburton
FREE WILL Thomas Pink
FREEMASONRY Andreas Önnerfors
FRENCH LITERATURE John D. Lyons
THE FRENCH REVOLUTION
  William Doyle
FREUD Anthony Storr
FUNDAMENTALISM Malise Ruthven

FUNGI Nicholas P. Money
THE FUTURE Jennifer M. Gidley
GALAXIES John Gribbin
GALILEO Stillman Drake
GAME THEORY Ken Binmore
GANDHI Bhikhu Parekh
GARDEN HISTORY Gordon Campbell
GENES Jonathan Slack
GENIUS Andrew Robinson
GENOMICS John Archibald
GEOFFREY CHAUCER David Wallace
GEOGRAPHY John Matthews
  and David Herbert
GEOLOGY Jan Zalasiewicz
GEOPHYSICS William Lowrie
GEOPOLITICS Klaus Dodds
GERMAN LITERATURE Nicholas Boyle
GERMAN PHILOSOPHY
  Andrew Bowie
GLACIATION David J. A. Evans
GLOBAL CATASTROPHES Bill McGuire
GLOBAL ECONOMIC HISTORY
  Robert C. Allen
GLOBALIZATION Manfred Steger
GOD John Bowker
GOETHE Ritchie Robertson
THE GOTHIC Nick Groom
GOVERNANCE Mark Bevir
GRAVITY Timothy Clifton
THE GREAT DEPRESSION AND
  THE NEW DEAL Eric Rauchway
HABERMAS James Gordon Finlayson
THE HABSBURG EMPIRE
  Martyn Rady
HAPPINESS Daniel M. Haybron
THE HARLEM RENAISSANCE
  Cheryl A. Wall
THE HEBREW BIBLE AS LITERATURE
  Tod Linafelt
HEGEL Peter Singer
HEIDEGGER Michael Inwood
THE HELLENISTIC AGE
  Peter Thonemann
HEREDITY John Waller
HERMENEUTICS Jens Zimmermann
HERODOTUS Jennifer T. Roberts
HIEROGLYPHS Penelope Wilson
HINDUISM Kim Knott
HISTORY John H. Arnold
THE HISTORY OF ASTRONOMY
  Michael Hoskin

THE HISTORY OF CHEMISTRY
    William H. Brock
THE HISTORY OF CHILDHOOD
    James Marten
THE HISTORY OF CINEMA
    Geoffrey Nowell-Smith
THE HISTORY OF LIFE
    Michael Benton
THE HISTORY OF MATHEMATICS
    Jacqueline Stedall
THE HISTORY OF MEDICINE
    William Bynum
THE HISTORY OF PHYSICS
    J. L. Heilbron
THE HISTORY OF TIME
    Leofranc Holford-Strevens
HIV AND AIDS Alan Whiteside
HOBBES Richard Tuck
HOLLYWOOD Peter Decherney
THE HOLY ROMAN EMPIRE
    Joachim Whaley
HOME Michael Allen Fox
HOMER Barbara Graziosi
HORMONES Martin Luck
HUMAN ANATOMY
    Leslie Klenerman
HUMAN EVOLUTION Bernard Wood
HUMAN RIGHTS Andrew Clapham
HUMANISM Stephen Law
HUME A. J. Ayer
HUMOUR Noël Carroll
THE ICE AGE Jamie Woodward
IDENTITY Florian Coulmas
IDEOLOGY Michael Freeden
THE IMMUNE SYSTEM
    Paul Klenerman
INDIAN CINEMA
    Ashish Rajadhyaksha
INDIAN PHILOSOPHY Sue Hamilton
THE INDUSTRIAL REVOLUTION
    Robert C. Allen
INFECTIOUS DISEASE Marta L. Wayne
    and Benjamin M. Bolker
INFINITY Ian Stewart
INFORMATION Luciano Floridi
INNOVATION Mark Dodgson
    and David Gann
INTELLECTUAL PROPERTY
    Siva Vaidhyanathan
INTELLIGENCE Ian J. Deary
INTERNATIONAL LAW Vaughan Lowe

INTERNATIONAL MIGRATION
    Khalid Koser
INTERNATIONAL RELATIONS
    Paul Wilkinson
INTERNATIONAL SECURITY
    Christopher S. Browning
IRAN Ali M. Ansari
ISLAM Malise Ruthven
ISLAMIC HISTORY Adam Silverstein
ISOTOPES Rob Ellam
ITALIAN LITERATURE
    Peter Hainsworth and David Robey
JESUS Richard Bauckham
JEWISH HISTORY David N. Myers
JOURNALISM Ian Hargreaves
JUDAISM Norman Solomon
JUNG Anthony Stevens
KABBALAH Joseph Dan
KAFKA Ritchie Robertson
KANT Roger Scruton
KEYNES Robert Skidelsky
KIERKEGAARD Patrick Gardiner
KNOWLEDGE Jennifer Nagel
THE KORAN Michael Cook
LAKES Warwick F. Vincent
LANDSCAPE ARCHITECTURE
    Ian H. Thompson
LANDSCAPES AND
    GEOMORPHOLOGY
    Andrew Goudie and Heather Viles
LANGUAGES Stephen R. Anderson
LATE ANTIQUITY Gillian Clark
LAW Raymond Wacks
THE LAWS OF THERMODYNAMICS
    Peter Atkins
LEADERSHIP Keith Grint
LEARNING Mark Haselgrove
LEIBNIZ Maria Rosa Antognazza
LEO TOLSTOY Liza Knapp
LIBERALISM Michael Freeden
LIGHT Ian Walmsley
LINCOLN Allen C. Guelzo
LINGUISTICS Peter Matthews
LITERARY THEORY Jonathan Culler
LOCKE John Dunn
LOGIC Graham Priest
LOVE Ronald de Sousa
MACHIAVELLI Quentin Skinner
MADNESS Andrew Scull
MAGIC Owen Davies
MAGNA CARTA Nicholas Vincent

MAGNETISM Stephen Blundell
MALTHUS Donald Winch
MAMMALS T. S. Kemp
MANAGEMENT John Hendry
MAO Delia Davin
MARINE BIOLOGY Philip V. Mladenov
THE MARQUIS DE SADE
John Phillips
MARTIN LUTHER Scott H. Hendrix
MARTYRDOM Jolyon Mitchell
MARX Peter Singer
MATERIALS Christopher Hall
MATHEMATICAL FINANCE
Mark H. A. Davis
MATHEMATICS Timothy Gowers
MATTER Geoff Cottrell
THE MEANING OF LIFE
Terry Eagleton
MEASUREMENT David Hand
MEDICAL ETHICS Michael Dunn
and Tony Hope
MEDICAL LAW Charles Foster
MEDIEVAL BRITAIN John Gillingham
and Ralph A. Griffiths
MEDIEVAL LITERATURE
Elaine Treharne
MEDIEVAL PHILOSOPHY
John Marenbon
MEMORY Jonathan K. Foster
METAPHYSICS Stephen Mumford
METHODISM William J. Abraham
THE MEXICAN REVOLUTION
Alan Knight
MICHAEL FARADAY
Frank A. J. L. James
MICROBIOLOGY
Nicholas P. Money
MICROECONOMICS Avinash Dixit
MICROSCOPY Terence Allen
THE MIDDLE AGES Miri Rubin
MILITARY JUSTICE Eugene R. Fidell
MILITARY STRATEGY
Antulio J. Echevarria II
MINERALS David Vaughan
MIRACLES Yujin Nagasawa
MODERN ARCHITECTURE
Adam Sharr
MODERN ART David Cottington
MODERN CHINA Rana Mitter
MODERN DRAMA
Kirsten E. Shepherd-Barr

MODERN FRANCE
Vanessa R. Schwartz
MODERN INDIA Craig Jeffrey
MODERN IRELAND Senia Pašeta
MODERN ITALY Anna Cento Bull
MODERN JAPAN
Christopher Goto-Jones
MODERN LATIN AMERICAN
LITERATURE
Roberto González Echevarría
MODERN WAR Richard English
MODERNISM Christopher Butler
MOLECULAR BIOLOGY Aysha Divan
and Janice A. Royds
MOLECULES Philip Ball
MONASTICISM Stephen J. Davis
THE MONGOLS Morris Rossabi
MOONS David A. Rothery
MORMONISM
Richard Lyman Bushman
MOUNTAINS Martin F. Price
MUHAMMAD Jonathan A. C. Brown
MULTICULTURALISM
Ali Rattansi
MULTILINGUALISM John C. Maher
MUSIC Nicholas Cook
MYTH Robert A. Segal
NAPOLEON David Bell
THE NAPOLEONIC WARS
Mike Rapport
NATIONALISM Steven Grosby
NATIVE AMERICAN LITERATURE
Sean Teuton
NAVIGATION Jim Bennett
NAZI GERMANY Jane Caplan
NELSON MANDELA Elleke Boehmer
NEOLIBERALISM Manfred Steger
and Ravi Roy
NETWORKS Guido Caldarelli
and Michele Catanzaro
THE NEW TESTAMENT
Luke Timothy Johnson
THE NEW TESTAMENT AS
LITERATURE Kyle Keefer
NEWTON Robert Iliffe
NIETZSCHE Michael Tanner
NINETEENTH-CENTURY BRITAIN
Christopher Harvie and
H. C. G. Matthew
THE NORMAN CONQUEST
George Garnett

NORTH AMERICAN INDIANS
    Theda Perdue and Michael D. Green
NORTHERN IRELAND
    Marc Mulholland
NOTHING Frank Close
NUCLEAR PHYSICS Frank Close
NUCLEAR POWER Maxwell Irvine
NUCLEAR WEAPONS
    Joseph M. Siracusa
NUMBERS Peter M. Higgins
NUTRITION David A. Bender
OBJECTIVITY Stephen Gaukroger
OCEANS Dorrik Stow
THE OLD TESTAMENT
    Michael D. Coogan
THE ORCHESTRA D. Kern Holoman
ORGANIC CHEMISTRY
    Graham Patrick
ORGANIZATIONS Mary Jo Hatch
ORGANIZED CRIME
    Georgios A. Antonopoulos and
    Georgios Papanicolaou
ORTHODOX CHRISTIANITY
    A. Edward Siecienski
PAGANISM Owen Davies
PAIN Rob Boddice
THE PALESTINIAN-ISRAELI
    CONFLICT Martin Bunton
PANDEMICS Christian W. McMillen
PARTICLE PHYSICS Frank Close
PAUL E. P. Sanders
PEACE Oliver P. Richmond
PENTECOSTALISM William K. Kay
PERCEPTION Brian Rogers
THE PERIODIC TABLE Eric R. Scerri
PHILOSOPHY Edward Craig
PHILOSOPHY IN THE
    ISLAMIC WORLD Peter Adamson
PHILOSOPHY OF LAW
    Raymond Wacks
PHILOSOPHY OF SCIENCE
    Samir Okasha
PHILOSOPHY OF RELIGION
    Tim Bayne
PHOTOGRAPHY Steve Edwards
PHYSICAL CHEMISTRY Peter Atkins
PHYSICS Sidney Perkowitz
PILGRIMAGE Ian Reader
PLAGUE Paul Slack
PLANETS David A. Rothery
PLANTS Timothy Walker
PLATE TECTONICS Peter Molnar
PLATO Julia Annas
POLITICAL PHILOSOPHY
    David Miller
POLITICS Kenneth Minogue
POPULISM Cas Mudde and
    Cristóbal Rovira Kaltwasser
POSTCOLONIALISM Robert Young
POSTMODERNISM Christopher Butler
POSTSTRUCTURALISM
    Catherine Belsey
POVERTY Philip N. Jefferson
PREHISTORY Chris Gosden
PRESOCRATIC PHILOSOPHY
    Catherine Osborne
PRIVACY Raymond Wacks
PROBABILITY John Haigh
PROGRESSIVISM Walter Nugent
PROJECTS Andrew Davies
PROTESTANTISM Mark A. Noll
PSYCHIATRY Tom Burns
PSYCHOANALYSIS Daniel Pick
PSYCHOLOGY Gillian Butler and
    Freda McManus
PSYCHOLOGY OF MUSIC
    Elizabeth Hellmuth Margulis
PSYCHOTHERAPY Tom Burns and
    Eva Burns-Lundgren
PUBLIC ADMINISTRATION
    Stella Z. Theodoulou and Ravi K. Roy
PUBLIC HEALTH Virginia Berridge
PURITANISM Francis J. Bremer
THE QUAKERS Pink Dandelion
QUANTUM THEORY
    John Polkinghorne
RACISM Ali Rattansi
RADIOACTIVITY Claudio Tuniz
RASTAFARI Ennis B. Edmonds
READING Belinda Jack
THE REAGAN REVOLUTION Gil Troy
REALITY Jan Westerhoff
THE REFORMATION Peter Marshall
RELATIVITY Russell Stannard
RELIGION IN AMERICA Timothy Beal
THE RENAISSANCE Jerry Brotton
RENAISSANCE ART
    Geraldine A. Johnson
REPTILES T.S. Kemp
REVOLUTIONS Jack A. Goldstone

RHETORIC Richard Toye
RISK Baruch Fischhoff and John Kadvany
RITUAL Barry Stephenson
RIVERS Nick Middleton
ROBOTICS Alan Winfield
ROCKS Jan Zalasiewicz
ROMAN BRITAIN Peter Salway
THE ROMAN EMPIRE
    Christopher Kelly
THE ROMAN REPUBLIC
    David M. Gwynn
ROMANTICISM Michael Ferber
ROUSSEAU Robert Wokler
RUSSELL A. C. Grayling
RUSSIAN HISTORY Geoffrey Hosking
RUSSIAN LITERATURE Catriona Kelly
THE RUSSIAN REVOLUTION
    S. A. Smith
SAINTS Simon Yarrow
SAVANNAS Peter A. Furley
SCEPTICISM Duncan Pritchard
SCHIZOPHRENIA Chris Frith and
    Eve Johnstone
SCHOPENHAUER
    Christopher Janaway
SCIENCE AND RELIGION
    Thomas Dixon
SCIENCE FICTION David Seed
THE SCIENTIFIC REVOLUTION
    Lawrence M. Principe
SCOTLAND Rab Houston
SECULARISM Andrew Copson
SEXUAL SELECTION Marlene Zuk
    and Leigh W. Simmons
SEXUALITY Véronique Mottier
SHAKESPEARE'S COMEDIES
    Bart van Es
SHAKESPEARE'S SONNETS
    AND POEMS Jonathan F. S. Post
SHAKESPEARE'S TRAGEDIES
    Stanley Wells
SIKHISM Eleanor Nesbitt
THE SILK ROAD James A. Millward
SLANG Jonathon Green
SLEEP Steven W. Lockley and
    Russell G. Foster
SOCIAL AND CULTURAL
    ANTHROPOLOGY
    John Monaghan and Peter Just
SOCIAL PSYCHOLOGY Richard J. Crisp

SOCIAL WORK Sally Holland and
    Jonathan Scourfield
SOCIALISM Michael Newman
SOCIOLINGUISTICS John Edwards
SOCIOLOGY Steve Bruce
SOCRATES C. C. W. Taylor
SOUND Mike Goldsmith
SOUTHEAST ASIA James R. Rush
THE SOVIET UNION Stephen Lovell
THE SPANISH CIVIL WAR
    Helen Graham
SPANISH LITERATURE Jo Labanyi
SPINOZA Roger Scruton
SPIRITUALITY Philip Sheldrake
SPORT Mike Cronin
STARS Andrew King
STATISTICS David J. Hand
STEM CELLS Jonathan Slack
STOICISM Brad Inwood
STRUCTURAL ENGINEERING
    David Blockley
STUART BRITAIN John Morrill
SUPERCONDUCTIVITY
    Stephen Blundell
SYMMETRY Ian Stewart
SYNAESTHESIA Julia Simner
SYNTHETIC BIOLOGY
    Jamie A. Davies
TAXATION Stephen Smith
TEETH Peter S. Ungar
TELESCOPES Geoff Cottrell
TERRORISM Charles Townshend
THEATRE Marvin Carlson
THEOLOGY David F. Ford
THINKING AND REASONING
    Jonathan St B. T. Evans
THOMAS AQUINAS Fergus Kerr
THOUGHT Tim Bayne
TIBETAN BUDDHISM
    Matthew T. Kapstein
TOCQUEVILLE Harvey C. Mansfield
TRAGEDY Adrian Poole
TRANSLATION Matthew Reynolds
THE TREATY OF VERSAILLES
    Michael S. Neiberg
THE TROJAN WAR Eric H. Cline
TRUST Katherine Hawley
THE TUDORS John Guy
TWENTIETH-CENTURY BRITAIN
    Kenneth O. Morgan

TYPOGRAPHY Paul Luna
THE UNITED NATIONS
    Jussi M. Hanhimäki
UNIVERSITIES AND COLLEGES
    David Palfreyman and Paul Temple
THE U.S. CONGRESS Donald A. Ritchie
THE U.S. CONSTITUTION
    David J. Bodenhamer
THE U.S. SUPREME COURT
    Linda Greenhouse
UTILITARIANISM
    Katarzyna de Lazari-Radek
    and Peter Singer
UTOPIANISM Lyman Tower Sargent
VETERINARY SCIENCE James Yeates
THE VIKINGS Julian D. Richards
VIRUSES Dorothy H. Crawford
VOLTAIRE Nicholas Cronk

WAR AND TECHNOLOGY
    Alex Roland
WATER John Finney
WAVES Mike Goldsmith
WEATHER Storm Dunlop
THE WELFARE STATE David Garland
WILLIAM SHAKESPEARE
    Stanley Wells
WITCHCRAFT Malcolm Gaskill
WITTGENSTEIN A. C. Grayling
WORK Stephen Fineman
WORLD MUSIC Philip Bohlman
THE WORLD TRADE
    ORGANIZATION Amrita Narlikar
WORLD WAR II Gerhard L. Weinberg
WRITING AND SCRIPT
    Andrew Robinson
ZIONISM Michael Stanislawski

Available soon:

PSYCHOPATHY Essi Viding
POETRY Bernard O'Donoghue
ENERGY SYSTEMS Nick Jenkins

TIDES David George Bowers
    and Emyr Martyn Roberts
DYNASTY Jeroen Duindam

For more information visit our website

www.oup.com/vsi/

Duncan Pritchard

SCEPTICISM

A Very Short Introduction

OXFORD
UNIVERSITY PRESS

OXFORD

UNIVERSITY PRESS

Great Clarendon Street, Oxford, OX2 6DP,
United Kingdom

Oxford University Press is a department of the University of Oxford.
It furthers the University's objective of excellence in research, scholarship,
and education by publishing worldwide. Oxford is a registered trade mark of
Oxford University Press in the UK and in certain other countries

Published in the United States of America by Oxford University Press
198 Madison Avenue, New York, NY 10016, United States of America

British Library Cataloguing in Publication Data
Data available

Library of Congress Control Number: 2019944354

ISBN 978-0-19-882916-4

Printed in Great Britain by
Ashford Colour Press Ltd, Gosport, Hampshire

For my parents,
Daisy and Les Pritchard

Contents

Acknowledgements xvii

List of illustrations xix

1 What is scepticism? 1

2 Is knowledge impossible? 23

3 Defending knowledge 47

4 Scepticism as a way of life 72

Further reading and references 97

Index 107

Acknowledgements

Scepticism is the issue that initially got me hooked on philosophy, and it's the topic that I find myself continually returning to. Inevitably, then, when I was first approached by Andrea Keegan at Oxford University Press about writing the book on scepticism for their *Very Short Introduction* series, I jumped at the chance. I am grateful to Jenny Nugee for her help preparing the manuscript, Deborah Protheroe for her assistance selecting images for the book, Joy Mellor for her sterling copyediting work, and to two anonymous reviewers for Oxford University Press who provided extensive comments on an earlier draft.

One of the challenges facing anyone who attempts to write about a contemporary philosophical topic for a general audience is to find a way to cut through the terminology that academic philosophy uses and get down to the fundamental issues. Fortune clearly smiled on the project in this regard, since around the time that Oxford University Press approached me I was given the opportunity to produce a MOOC (= Massive Open Online Course) for the University of California, Irvine (UCI). Working on these projects in tandem, both aimed at a wider audience, got me thinking about how sceptical ideas are often used—I would say *mis*used, as I explain in the book—to motivate certain problematic relativistic positions in public debate. More specifically, it made me see how an introduction to scepticism could relate sceptical themes to contemporary issues, and thereby make these issues relevant to the non-specialist. You can find this online course, and enrol (at no cost), on the Coursera platform. For more details, go to: https://www.coursera.org/learn/skepticism. (See also the sibling MOOC on 'Relativism' that was produced as part of this project, led by my colleague Annalisa Coliva and which will be launched on the Coursera platform shortly.)

I've had an enormous amount of support for this book from UCI via the production of the MOOC that goes with it. This included Douglas Haynes, Vice Provost for Academic Equity, Diversity and Inclusion, Gary Matkin, Dean of Continuing Education, and Megan Wanlin Linos, Director of Learning Experience Design and Online Education in the Division of Teaching Excellence and Innovation, who all supported the project from the off, along with everyone involved in the mechanics of producing the course, especially LaDawna Minnis and Kristoffer Velasquez. Thanks also to the distinguished UCI academics who participated in the filming, as part of two panel discussions devoted to the issues arising from Chapters 1 and 4. These were Howard Gilman, Chancellor of UCI and a prominent defender of free speech on campus; Julia Lupton, Associate Dean for Research in the School of Humanities and all-round Shakespeare-supremo; Michael Dennin, Vice Provost for Teaching and Learning, physicist and advocate for popularizing science; and leading bioroboticist, David Reinkensmeyer.

Finally, thanks to my wife Mandi and our lovely boys, Alexander and Ethan. Mandi cast her astute critical eye over the manuscript, making many valuable suggestions. This is also the first of my books to have been read by Alexander, who looked over an early draft—hopefully this won't be his last!

D. H. P.
Irvine, USA
April 2019

List of illustrations

1   Climate change **3**
iStock.com/Anne Belden.

2   Post-truth/fact politics **4**
U.S. National Park Service.

3   Relativism and art **10**
State Hermitage Museum, St.
Petersburg. © DEA/E. Lessing/De
Agostini Editore/age fotostock.

4   The absurd **21**
Museo del Prado, Madrid. © Fine Art
Images/Heritage Image/age
fotostock.

5   The brain in a vat **31**
Tim Vernon/Science Photo Library.

6   Scepticism at the movies **32**
Warner Bros/Kobal/Shutterstock.

7   Hands **52**
Rijksmuseum, Amsterdam.

8   Hinges **65**
Jozef Jankola/Shutterstock.com.

9   Faith and doubt **68**
Sanssouci Picture Gallery, Potsdam.
© Artepics/Alamy/age fotostock.

10 Faith versus science **75**
Private collection.
© DEA/U. Marzani/De Agostini
Editore/age fotostock.

11 Aristotle **79**
MidoSemsem/Shutterstock.com.

12 Conviction and public
reason **90**
The Art Archive/Shutterstock.

Chapter 1
What is scepticism?

Introducing scepticism

In a nutshell, scepticism is about *doubt* in that to be sceptical
about something is to have doubts about it. Scepticism can apply
to lots of different things: one can be sceptical about a person
(e.g. the proverbial used-car sales person), a topic (e.g. horoscope
predictions), and even objects (e.g. one might be sceptical that
one's clapped-out air conditioning is going to last the summer).
What these different forms of scepticism have in common is that
one is concerned about whether one can rely on the thing in
question, whether it is the advice of the used-car sales person, the
predictions made by the horoscope, or the effectiveness of the air
conditioning. In short, scepticism undermines *belief* (belief that
what the car sales person is telling you is correct, belief that the air
conditioning unit will last the summer, and so on), and so this is
what we will be focusing upon here.

A certain degree of scepticism is often a good thing. Indeed, we
talk about the importance of having a 'healthy scepticism', where
this means not simply accepting whatever one is told. Scepticism
in this sense is the antidote to *gullibility*, and surely no-one wants
to be gullible. Some things warrant scepticism after all. Take the
example I just mentioned of horoscopes. These predictions are
notoriously problematic in that they are either very specific, in

which case they are often wrong, or more often they are so general that they would fit any eventuality, in which case there is no clear sense in which they are ever right. Moreover, we also know that there is no scientific basis for astrology—scientists long ago abandoned astrology in favour of astronomy, which unlike astrology is an accepted scientific discipline. So there are excellent grounds for being sceptical about the reliability of horoscopes.

A healthy scepticism can also prevent us from being taken in by those who want to deceive us. For example, since we know that used-car sales people have a motive for wanting us to buy a car at the highest price possible, we know that we should take what they say with a pinch of salt and not simply accept it completely at face-value. More generally, if someone we don't know well tells us something that seems at first blush to be rather incredible—for example, that the Queen of England has just been arrested for shoplifting—then our sceptical instinct should kick in to ensure that we don't simply take this testimony on trust. That's not to say that we should never accept incredible testimony of this kind, but only that we should always demand extra grounds in such cases (e.g. we might want to switch on the news to verify this astonishing tale).

But this type of quite specific scepticism can also easily drift into something more extreme and generalized. It is scepticism of this kind—what is known as *radical scepticism*—that will be of particular interest to us. For example, what are we to make of the contemporary trend in some aspects of public life to be sceptical about science itself, such as concerning the scientific consensus about human-caused climate change (Figure 1)? Notice how this kind of scepticism is very different to scepticism about horoscopes. In the latter case, the scepticism is grounded in a belief in the reliability of science. And that seems legitimate precisely because we regard science as being a paradigmatic way of getting to the truth about the world around us. But when one is sceptical about science itself, then of course that kind of scepticism cannot be

1. **Climate change. There is a clear scientific consensus regarding the existence of human-caused climate change, including its relevance for at least some contemporary weather-related events (such as the 2017 California wildfires pictured here), but that hasn't prevented some very high-profile political figures from denying this.**

grounded in science. If we reject the authority of science to tell us about the world around us, however, then what will be our basis for belief in this regard? The worry is that a healthy scepticism is here morphing into a generalized scepticism that is an entirely different beast.

Here's another way of putting the point. There can be all kinds of good reasons why it might be right to be sceptical about particular claims, such as regarding what horoscopes or used-car sales people tell us. Such *localized* sceptical doubt is, however, grounded in what we know, such as our knowledge of the unscientific nature of horoscopes and the motivations of used-car sales people. But once we shift from a localized sceptical doubt to one that is much more general—as when we become sceptical of scientific claims *en masse*—then it is hard to make sense of how our scepticism is grounded in what we know at all. For whatever we might cite as reasons for this doubt, wouldn't they be equally in

3

doubt too? The worry is that rather than being grounded in something that we can rely upon, as a localized sceptical doubt might be, a generalized or wholesale sceptical doubt becomes instead completely free-floating.

When scepticism of this more radical kind takes root in our public life, then it has all kinds of practical ramifications, many of them not particularly appealing. One consequence is a lack of concern for accuracy and the truth. Think, for example, of such contemporary phenomena as 'false facts' and 'post-truth politics' (Figure 2), whereby people in public life utter manifest falsehoods seemingly with impunity. A radical scepticism effectively licenses such phenomena, since once everything is open to doubt, then

2. Post-truth/fact politics. A debate broke out after Donald Trump's 2017 presidential inauguration about whether the official government photos had been edited to make the crowd look larger than it was, so that it wouldn't compare badly with previous inaugurations (or was this just a case of 'alternative facts', as one of Trump's advisors described it at the time?). This picture compares the crowd in 2017 with that present at Barack Obama's 2013 inauguration (shown left).

there is nothing that is accepted as true, and hence what's true starts to drop out of the equation altogether.

In particular, once a concern for truth and accuracy is lost, then a radical sceptical doubt gives way to a prevailing *relativism* about truth. This is the view that the truth is just simply whatever someone says it is. For example, one camp endorses the scientific consensus that climate change is human-caused, whereas another camp argues that these scientists are all part of a global conspiracy to deceive the public. According to relativism, *both* camps can be right, since truth is relative to one's subjective opinion.

It might initially seem liberating to shake off a concern for truth and accuracy in this way, and to allow that opposing groups can both be right, but this is an illusion. For notice that to say that both camps in a dispute are right is as empty as saying that they are both wrong. Once you abandon the idea of accuracy, then it doesn't matter any more what's true and what isn't. But getting things right *should* matter to us.

In order to see this, just consider something that you take to be extremely important. For example, imagine that you are charged with a serious crime that you didn't commit. Wouldn't it matter a great deal to you that the truth was brought to light, and hence that you were acquitted? And wouldn't it appal you if, even after being acquitted, those who accused you continued to maintain, in a relativistic spirit, that, contrary to the evidence produced in favour of your innocence at your trial, it was just as much 'true' that you committed the crime in question? You would surely regard this as an injustice, and you would be right to do so. But that just goes to show that the truth counts, and that means the truth in the sense of what actually is the case. But of course there can't be multiple inconsistent accounts of what is actually the case. Either you did the crime or you didn't. And if you didn't, then anyone who says otherwise is saying something false, not saying something true that is relative to their subjective opinion.

So how do we go about differentiating, in a principled way, between a healthy scepticism which targets only specific claims, and a more generalized scepticism that has the pernicious consequences just noted? This is one of the key questions that we will be exploring. To this end, we will first be examining a famous philosophical argument that purports to show that it is impossible to know anything. If that argument succeeds, then it would provide a basis for the generalized scepticism we have just looked at. But, as we will see, there are in fact a number of responses to scepticism of this kind. We will also be considering an influential philosophical account of human flourishing which puts the virtues centre-stage, including the intellectual virtues, and considering how a localized form of scepticism can be grounded in these virtues. Very roughly, the virtues are character traits that promote human flourishing, where the intellectual virtues are a sub-set of those traits that are specifically concerned with intellectual ends like accuracy and truth. We will be looking at how a sceptical attitude can be embedded within an account of the intellectual virtues, in order to find a way to determine when one's scepticism is healthy and when it isn't.

Truth, relativism, and fallibility

In the last section we encountered relativism about truth. This is the idea that what is true is relative to one's subjective opinion, so that if your opinion is in conflict with someone else's opinion then—no problem!—you can *both* be right. We noted that relativism about truth is not all it's cracked up to be, not least because if everyone is right, then everyone is just as much wrong too. The point is that if the idea of truth capturing whether a viewpoint is accurate or not is lost, then it really doesn't matter any more whether that viewpoint is true or false. And yet we clearly do care about getting things right, particularly when this concerns something of personal importance, such as whether one is wrongly found guilty of a serious crime. Or, to take another example, if a doctor is about to operate on you, I think you would care a great deal whether the surgery they were about to perform was based on accepted medical practice rather than just being the doctor's subjective opinion.

But if relativism about truth is such a bad idea, then why might some people be attracted to it? I think there are several reasons. One reason might be that *some* things are simply a matter of subjective opinion. What foods you like, what you find funny, your favourite film, and so on. These are all just matters of subjective opinion. In particular, there's nothing odd about the fact that I hate sweet foods, but that most people really like sweet foods. But that some things—matters of taste, essentially—are just a matter of subjective opinion doesn't mean that everything is.

Suppose, for example, that a scientist claims to have discovered a new planet. Either what they say is true, in which case the planet they describe exists, or it's false, in which case the planet they describe doesn't exist. Opinions don't come into the matter at all. And that's precisely because when we talk about whether something is true, we want to know whether it is actually the case, and not merely what someone thinks might be the case.

(By the way, there is still truth even when we are talking about subjective matters of taste, such as what foods one prefers. Take the claim that I can't stand the taste of sweet foods. It is purely a matter of subjective opinion that I don't like sweet foods, unlike most other people. But it is *not* a matter of subjective opinion that *it's true* that I don't like sweet foods, any more than it's a matter of subjective opinion that it's true that other people tend to like them. As in the case just described with the planet, either I do like sweet foods or I don't. If I don't like sweet foods, then the claim that I don't is true; otherwise it is false. And there's nothing relative or subjective about that.)

Another reason why some people might be attracted to relativism is that it can superficially seem to be liberating, and even a way of respecting the views of those we don't agree with. Rather than having to take sides in a debate, one can now just say that both parties are right. Isn't that a way of respecting the views of everyone concerned? But notice that this isn't to respect the other person's views at all. After all, they weren't saying that this was their subjective opinion, but that it was true—that is, such that they were right and the other party was wrong. In saying that they have merely claimed a relative truth, however, we are effectively saying that what they have claimed is not true at all, at least not as they meant it. After all, they weren't saying that this was just their subjective opinion, but that it was actually (i.e. objectively) true. In particular, they were claiming that they were right and the other person's views were wrong, not that they were both saying something true (albeit in a relativistic way).

What applies to other people's opinions applies with even more force to one's own. Think about your most cherished beliefs, such as your ethical, political, or religious convictions. Now contrast these cherished beliefs with claims that are merely a matter of your own subjective opinion. You clearly think the former are true, which is why you have such conviction in them. But what comfort would you get in discovering that 'true' here just means your own subjective opinion and nothing more? After all, you don't think that your deepest convictions are just matters of taste, such as whether you like (or dislike) sweet foods.

Suppose, for example, that you come across someone who has completely different political views to you. Perhaps you are in favour of western liberal democracy, while they favour a totalitarian state ruled by a strong leader. If this disagreement is just about a matter of taste, then there would be nothing to disagree about, any more than there is any point in me 'disagreeing' with someone over whether sweet foods taste nice (they simply don't for me, but do for others). And yet there clearly is something substantive here worth disagreeing about, as the political organization of society has all sorts of practical implications for the lives that we lead. This simply isn't the sort of issue where one can casually shrug one's shoulders, as you might if I told you that I didn't like sweet foods!

Yet another reason why I think some people are initially attracted to relativism is because of the inherent *fallibility* of our judgements. What I mean by this is that even our best judgements can sometimes be mistaken. Put another way, we are not infallible creatures. This is true even of science. The best, most grounded scientific theories of the day could give way, over time, to better scientific theories that completely replace the earlier proposals. (The idea that the sun orbited the earth, rather than vice versa, was once a widely held claim, after all.) But if it is always possible that we might be wrong, then how confident can we be that we are ever right? In particular, how confident can we be that what we believe is really true, as opposed to merely being a subjective opinion that could turn out to be false? Accordingly, why not jettison the idea of truth as objective and instead treat it as merely relative (Figure 3)?

There are several points that we need to tease out here. The first thing to notice is that this line of reasoning is primarily motivating scepticism rather than relativism. This is thus a good juncture to remind ourselves of the difference. Recall that scepticism concerns doubt, primarily doubt about what is true. So construed, the sceptic is not proposing that truth is just subjective opinion in the way that the relativist is. Indeed, what is motivating scepticism is rather the worry that our beliefs might not be true in an *objective* sense. As we noted earlier, however, scepticism can slide into relativism if the former becomes extensive enough. If we are inclined to doubt everything, then we might be tempted to think that there is no such thing as an objective truth, and hence that everything is just a matter of subjective opinion instead.

The general worry about our fallibility is primarily motivating scepticism rather than relativism because it is giving us a reason

3. Relativism and art. While relativism about truth might have
pernicious social and political consequences, relativistic ideas more
generally energized the art world in the first half of the 20th century,
as this painting ('Portrait of a Philosopher', 1915) by the Russian
avant-garde artist Lyubov Popova (1889–1924) illustrates.

to doubt even those things that we are most confident of. After all, people have been very confident of things in the past (such as that the sun orbited the earth) and have turned out to be mistaken. Accordingly, we seem to have a reason to doubt everything we believe. The connection to relativism comes in only indirectly, via the point we just noted about how once one's scepticism becomes extensive enough, then it seems to invite relativism.

Crucially, however, while there are some good arguments for scepticism—indeed, we are going to be considering one influential argument in this regard soon—the appeal to our fallibility is not a good basis to be generally sceptical about the truth of our beliefs. Yes, it is always possible that you are mistaken. But that in itself is not a good reason to be sceptical about everything you believe (or even most of what you believe). What you need is rather some specific reason to think that you are mistaken in this particular case.

In order to see this, consider some everyday scenarios. Take, for example, the question of whether a particular tree is an oak. If I am the person making the judgement, then there are some grounds for scepticism about it, as I'm not very reliable when it comes to identifying types of tree. But compare this case with someone making the very same judgement who is a qualified arborist with a long history of working with trees of different kinds. Sure, it's still possible that they might be mistaken, but unlike my judgement that the tree is an oak, this isn't a serious possibility at all, as it would frankly be incredible that someone with this level of expertise should misidentify something so common as an oak tree. The point is that mere fallibility alone is not a good basis for doubt; rather one needs some specific reason to think that one might be mistaken in this particular case.

We can also see this point in action when we look at scientific practice. Scientists openly recognize that their enterprise is fallible. Indeed, this fallibility is built into the structure of science.

The fact that even the best confirmed scientific theories could nonetheless be false is what leads scientists to be constantly testing their theories. Experimental results are repeated by other scientists to check for anomalies, experimental trials are conducted 'blind' in order to screen-out any possible bias in the interpretation of the results, predictions are extracted from scientific theories and then tested, and so on. The point of all of this is to expose scientific theorizing to as much examination as is feasible in order to ensure that it is as accurate as possible. Significantly, however, when a theory has been road-tested in this fashion, then while it is still possible that it might be wrong, there isn't any longer any particular reason to be sceptical about it. Again, then, we find that mere fallibility alone is not a good basis for doubt.

What is knowledge?

Up until now we have been focusing on our beliefs about the truth. But we don't just want to believe the truth, we want to *know* it. Relatedly, if the sceptic is able to get us to doubt what we believe, then they thereby ensure that we don't have knowledge, since if we don't even believe it, then we can't know it. And that really is the ultimate goal of the sceptic: to convince us that we don't know much, if anything, of what we take ourselves to know, and thereby in the process get us to doubt everything that we hitherto took to be true.

The reason why knowing involves more than just believing is that one can form one's beliefs in all kinds of inappropriate ways. For example, a lucky guess is not knowledge. Or, to take another kind of case, imagine someone who is completely gullible in that they believe everything that they are told, no matter how ridiculous. Most of what they are told is false, let us say, but every now and again they are told something true. Since they believe everything they are told, amongst the many falsehoods that they believe are also the odd truths. But clearly these true beliefs do not amount to knowledge. One cannot gain knowledge by believing whatever one is told, even if one happens to believe something true as a result. Gullibility is not a route to knowledge, even if it chances on the truth.

So knowledge demands more than just true belief. Before we ask ourselves what else is required for knowledge over and above true belief, let us pause for a moment to consider what it means for knowledge to demand *at least* true belief.

The first thing to notice is that we are here talking about a particular kind of knowledge, what is known as *propositional* knowledge. As the name suggests, this is knowledge of a proposition, where a proposition is a statement that describes things as being a certain way. For example, that Paris is the capital of France, or that the square of 2 is 4. When we believe that something is the case (e.g. that Paris is the capital of France), what we are believing is a proposition. Thus, when we know what we believe, what we know is a true proposition.

Not all forms of knowledge are propositional. For example, consider ability knowledge, or *know-how*. I know how to ride a bicycle, how to swim, how to wire a plug, and many more things besides. Ability knowledge is clearly very different from propositional knowledge. While I know how to ride a bicycle, for instance, I couldn't tell you what it is, exactly, that I'm doing when I'm riding my bike. And a lot of ability knowledge is like that, if you think about it. Knowing how to do something is often very different to knowing a bunch of propositions related to that activity. In any case, when we say that there's more to knowledge than merely true belief, we are clearly talking about a kind of knowledge that is propositional, just as belief is propositional.

Next, consider the claim that knowledge requires *true* belief. Can there not be false knowledge (i.e. knowledge of false propositions)? It is certainly the case that someone can quite reasonably suppose they have knowledge and yet what they think they know is false. This was the situation that many people were in centuries ago when they quite reasonably thought that the sun orbited the earth. But thinking that you know, even reasonably thinking that you know, is not the same as actually knowing. Since it's not the case that the sun orbits the earth, then none of those people centuries ago who believed this actually knew what they believed; they merely thought that they did.

Notice that even though knowledge does demand truth (i.e. true belief), it doesn't thereby demand infallibility or even certainty. For example, a lot of our knowledge of the world around us is gained via our senses, such as by seeing, hearing, touching, and so forth—this is known as *perceptual knowledge*. Our senses are clearly fallible in that sometimes they deceive us. Optical illusions might trick us into seeing something that isn't there (e.g. as when a straight stick looks bent when placed underwater). Similarly, when under the influence of drugs one might have hallucinations. The fallibility of our senses does not prevent us from having perceptual knowledge, however—that is, knowledge that is acquired via our senses. For while you can't come to perceptually know that there is an oasis before you by having a hallucination to this effect, this doesn't mean that in ordinary conditions when your (fallible) perceptual faculties are working just fine they can't deliver knowledge. As we pointed out above when we discussed fallibility in the context of relativism, that we sometimes make mistakes is not a good basis to doubt everything we believe. For the same reason, it is also not a good basis to doubt whether we know anything either. That our knowledge is fallible does not mean that it is not bona fide knowledge nonetheless.

The same goes for certainty. I may be completely certain of the things that I know, but this isn't required, and often it isn't the case anyway. Right now, for example, I believe that my car is parked outside of my house. That's where I parked it earlier (something that I clearly remember), and I live in an area where car theft is unusual. Plus, only I have the keys to drive it (and I have them in my pocket). Thus the likelihood that the car is not presently parked outside on my drive is very low. If my belief is true, and my car is presently parked outside my house, then I think we would grant that this is something that I know. But am I completely certain of this claim? Well, while I am fairly confident of it, I don't think I would say that I am completely certain. After all, it has been some hours since I last saw my car on the drive, and although unlikely there are various scenarios that are not completely far-fetched whereby something has happened to it in the interim (not least that it has been stolen). That one's belief isn't completely certain does not entail that it fails to amount to knowledge.

So while knowledge demands truth, it doesn't demand infallibility or certainty. This means that the sceptics who seek to deprive us of knowledge need to do much more than show that our beliefs are acquired in fallible ways, or that we often are not completely certain of what we believe. So how do they motivate their sceptical doubt?

We noted a moment ago that knowledge demands more than just mere true belief. This is a good juncture to revisit that claim, because it is in the gap between knowledge and mere true belief that scepticism is able to gain some leverage. We noted above that mere true belief can be gained in all kinds of haphazard and inappropriate ways—for example, through mere gullibility. In such cases it wouldn't amount to knowledge. What would it take to turn a true belief into knowledge? There are various competing proposals on this score offered by contemporary epistemologists, but the general idea is that knowledge at the very least requires a true belief that is *grounded in good reasons*.

In particular, knowledge requires good reasons for thinking that the belief in question is true. The reason for this caveat is that there can be good reasons for believing a proposition which aren't thereby good reasons for thinking that what you believe is true. Imagine that someone has put a gun to your head and tells you that they will shoot you unless you believe in the existence of alien life. In such a scenario you clearly have a good reason to believe in the existence of alien life, since it's the only way to avoid being shot and killed. But that someone will shoot you if you don't believe that there is alien life is not a good reason to believe that it's true that alien life exists. It is rather a merely *prudential reason* to believe what you do—that is, something which it would be expedient for you to believe, given that you wish to stay alive.

In contrast, if scientists discovered that there is alien life and reported their discovery, then one would now have a good reason for believing that it's true that there is alien life. The scientists, after all, know what they are talking about in this regard, will have made appropriate observations, collected and verified supporting evidence for this claim, and so on. Reasons for thinking that a belief is true are known as *epistemic* reasons. (This is because the area of philosophy that is concerned with truth, knowledge, and such like is called *epistemology*, with its practitioners known as *epistemologists*.) When we talk about knowledge being true belief that is grounded in good reasons, it is epistemic reasons that we specifically have in mind—that is, reasons for thinking that the belief is question is true.

It is good reasons of this kind that are precisely missing when it comes to someone forming their beliefs through guesswork or mere gullibility. If one's true belief is just down to guesswork, then one has no good reasons at all for believing what one does, epistemic or otherwise. The gullible person may *think* that they have good reasons for believing what they do. This is what someone told them, after all, and they think that one should believe everything one is told, no matter how fantastical. But of course their reasons for believing what they do are not good epistemic reasons, since being willing to believe whatever one is told is not a good way to form true beliefs.

We can make this point crystal clear by comparing this way of forming a belief with someone who isn't at all gullible, and who hence forms their belief via testimony in an epistemically appropriate manner—for example, by being careful about whose testimony they accept, reflecting on the plausibility of what they have been told, and so on. Imagine, for example, someone who believes that there is alien life because they have listened to the testimony from the scientists, which was widely reported in all the main reputable news outlets. Such a person, if asked why they believe what they do, will be able to offer all kinds of good epistemic reasons in support of their belief. For instance, they could say that the person who told them is someone they know to be reliable about the relevant subject matter (which is true, as the scientists who work in this field know that their reputations depend on asserting only what the scientific evidence supports). They could also point out that the story is running on reputable news outlets, outlets that are renowned for checking their sources, and so on.

So while gullibility is not a route to knowledge, even when it results in a true belief, one can gain knowledge from someone else's testimony so long as one acquires one's true belief in a careful fashion. In particular, it is being careful about how one forms one's belief that will generate the good epistemic reasons that set this belief apart from a groundless belief that is formed via gullibility. And so long as the true belief is appropriately grounded in epistemic reasons, then it can amount to knowledge.

We can now see how one might go about motivating sceptical doubt. The idea is to show that one does not have good epistemic reasons in support of one's beliefs, and hence that one lacks knowledge. If that's right, then one's beliefs, even if true, are no better than someone who forms their beliefs in a completely gullible fashion (or, e.g., via mere guesswork).

A crucial point to notice here is that when sceptical doubt is motivated in this way it is not being claimed that one's beliefs are false. Indeed, for all the sceptic has claimed, one's beliefs might be entirely true. The point is rather that those beliefs do not enjoy good epistemic grounds, and hence don't amount to knowledge. This point is important since it illustrates that scepticism need not be targeted at the truth of our beliefs at all. Relatedly, going back to our earlier discussion about relativism, offering a relativistic account of truth, such that the truth is relative to one's subjective opinion, wouldn't have any bearing at all on the sceptical problem under this construal (even if we could find a way to make relativism coherent). The radical sceptic is saying that we lack knowledge of an objective truth, which is compatible with one having objectively true beliefs that don't amount to knowledge, and for that matter also with having subjectively true beliefs that don't amount to knowledge. Relativism would thus be entirely irrelevant to sceptical doubt that is targeted specifically at knowledge of objective truths in this way.

Recall too some of our other points from earlier. In particular, remember we noted that sceptical doubt wouldn't be very interesting if it was motivated via the claim that we need to be infallible or completely certain, as knowledge doesn't demand either. The same applies to scepticism that is focused specifically at our epistemic reasons. One can have good epistemic reasons for believing something true, and thereby have knowledge, even if those reasons are fallible, and even if those reasons do not suffice to make one completely certain. Indeed, in the case we just gave of someone who properly forms their belief that alien life exists by listening to the testimony of scientists, the epistemic reasons are hardly infallible, and our agent is unlikely to be completely certain of what they believe on this basis. Even so, they can come to have knowledge via forming their true belief in this way.

Remember too that we noted above that it is not enough to motivate sceptical doubt to argue that there is a mere possibility that one is mistaken. Just as knowledge can be acquired in a fallible way, so one can have genuine knowledge even when there is a remote possibility of error. What undermines knowledge are *serious* possibilities of error rather than *mere* possibilities of error. Forming one's beliefs via gullibility involves a serious possibility of error, as if one believes everything one is told, no matter how ridiculous, then one is bound to end up believing falsehoods. But forming a scientific belief by listening to the testimony of scientific experts, while inevitably fallible, does not involve a serious risk of error, and hence can be a route to knowledge.

So we are going to be considering a type of sceptical doubt that is directed at the epistemic grounds we have for our beliefs. Scepticism of this kind claims that we don't have adequate grounds for our beliefs, and hence we lack knowledge. This claim is entirely compatible with our beliefs being true, and so the sceptic isn't obliged to argue that they aren't true. But the sceptic does need to show that their scepticism doesn't presuppose that knowledge is infallible or that they are completely certain of what they believe. Relatedly, they need to demonstrate that they are appealing to a serious possibility of error, and not merely noting that there is a possibility, however remote, that they might be mistaken. As we will see, even given these constraints, there is a way of motivating sceptical doubt that satisfies all these conditions.

Scepticism and the absurd

Before we turn to considering this form of sceptical doubt, however, we will close this chapter by considering why it might matter to us that we do have the widespread knowledge that we take ourselves to have. Could we coherently accept the radical sceptical contention that we don't know very much with equanimity? I don't think so. This is a topic that we are going to explore more fully in Chapter 4, so for now I will just make some preliminary remarks in this regard.

Imagine that the sceptic is right and you don't know very much. Put this way, the claim might seem very abstract, but it's relatively straightforward to bring out the seismic practical ramifications of what the sceptic is contending. Think about it. You don't know that your parents are your parents. You don't know that your friends are your friends. You don't know anything about your past, about those cherished events that you seem to recall, or those achievements that you are so proud of. And so on. For all you know, none of these people exist and none of these events ever happened.

Indeed, as we will see in Chapter 2, the radical sceptic isn't just claiming that you lack knowledge, but rather, more specifically, that you lack any good epistemic reason for believing what you do. So it's not as if one can counter the radical sceptic by maintaining that while one lacks knowledge one does have good (epistemic) reasons for believing what one does, since if the sceptic is right then one doesn't even have the latter. That is, it's not just that you don't know that (say) your parents are your parents, but that you have no good (epistemic) reason for thinking that they are your parents—that is, *no reason at all for thinking that it's true* that the people you believe are your parents actually are your parents. And what goes here for your belief about your parents will apply to any belief concerning something that you care about.

Once we understand what scepticism means in practice, it should be easy to see why conceding the sceptical conclusion is so problematic. Indeed, wouldn't living a life on this basis make one's existence *absurd*, and thus *meaningless*? There are lots of ways that life could be meaningless. For example, consider the life of Sisyphus, who in Greek mythology was condemned to roll a large rock up a hill only to watch it roll back down again for all eternity

4. The absurd. There are many ways that our lives could be meaningless, one of which is that they could be completely pointless, such as the life that Sisyphus, a figure from Greek mythology (here depicted by Titian, c.1548), was condemned to lead.

(Figure 4). Sisyphus's life is meaningless because it is completely pointless. If scepticism were true, then this would be a different way that one's life could be meaningless, where rather than being pointless it would be senseless. For how could one's existence make any sense if one lacks knowledge of even the most basic facts about one's life? In particular, why should one care about anything if one doesn't have any reason to think that it's real?

We will return to this point later on, but for now I just want
to register the fact that radical scepticism appears to have
devastating consequences for the meaningfulness of our own lives.
It is in this sense an *existential* problem. If that's right, then
even if we set aside the pernicious social consequences of radical
scepticism that we noted earlier, it would remain a difficulty
that needs to be taken seriously due to how it threatens to make
our existences absurd.

Chapter 2
Is knowledge impossible?

In this chapter we are going to be looking at an influential argument that purports to show that we do not know much of what we take ourselves to know. If this argument works, then it licenses a radical sceptical doubt. Recall that in Chapter 1 we noted the difference between a localized sceptical doubt, which is concerned with only doubting certain specific claims, with a more generalized, or *radical*, sceptical doubt which calls much of our knowledge into doubt *en masse*. As we saw, there can be all kinds of good reasons why we should be sceptical about specific matters, and hence localized scepticism can be perfectly healthy from an intellectual point of view. It is rather the radical form of sceptical doubt that seems to be intellectually problematic. Indeed, we noted that once it takes root it has the tendency to generate all kinds of ills for public life, whereby people don't care any more what is true and what isn't. Even worse, we observed that radical scepticism has the potential to make one's life meaningless.

We also saw in Chapter 1, however, that motivating radical sceptical doubt of this kind is not straightforward. For example, it is not enough to merely appeal to the fact that we are sometimes mistaken, or more generally to simply note that we are fallible creatures. As we made clear, knowledge doesn't demand infallibility, and so that we have bona fide knowledge is entirely compatible with the fact that we are sometimes mistaken.

Relatedly, it is not enough to note that we are often not completely certain of the things that we believe, since knowledge doesn't demand complete certainty either.

If radical sceptical doubt cannot be motivated in these ways, then how might we motivate it? This is where the argument that we are going to consider comes in. The point of this kind of sceptical argument is to show that we don't have any good reasons for thinking that our beliefs are true.

Remember that we called reasons of this kind *epistemic* reasons, and contrasted them with merely *prudential* reasons. We have a prudential reason for believing something when it would be *useful* for us to believe it, regardless of whether it is true. Epistemic reasons, in contrast, are specifically reasons for thinking that the belief in question is true. It is epistemic reasons in support of our true beliefs that we need if we are to know what we believe. Accordingly, the radical sceptical argument that we will be examining will be claiming that we lack reasons of this specific kind in support of our beliefs.

Remember too that a sceptical argument that is focused on the epistemic reasons for our beliefs is not concerned with whether our beliefs are true. That is, scepticism of this kind is not claiming that our beliefs are generally false, but rather that they don't generally amount to knowledge (because they are not supported by good epistemic reasons). But our beliefs could be generally true and yet fail to amount to knowledge (just as someone who is completely gullible, and who hence doesn't know very much, might nonetheless have lots of true beliefs). Whether our beliefs are true, and whether, even if true, they amount to knowledge, are distinct issues.

Cartesian scepticism

With all this in mind, let's start constructing our argument for radical sceptical doubt. This is a contemporary radical sceptical argument that is rooted in the work of René Descartes (1596–1650), especially in his *Meditations on First Philosophy*. As such, this form of scepticism is standardly described as *Cartesian*, although it departs from the particular sceptical argument that Descartes offered in some crucial respects. (It is also often called *external world scepticism*, for reasons that will become apparent).

Note that Descartes wasn't himself a radical sceptic, and he certainly wasn't trying to convince anyone to embrace radical sceptical conclusions. His interest in radical scepticism was rather *methodological*. In particular, he wanted to find secure foundations for knowledge by employing a 'method of doubt'—that is, doubting as many of his beliefs as he possibly could. The point of his use of radical scepticism is thus as a kind of extreme 'stress test' applied to our system of belief. Descartes thought that in this way he could find the indubitable, and thereby *certain*, fixed-points in this system onto which our knowledge can be founded. In particular, if we can trace our knowledge back to such epistemically secure foundations, then we can be assured that it is thereby immune to sceptical challenges. This sort of epistemological project is thus known as *foundationalism*, and as such it should be clear it is meant to be a decidedly *anti*-sceptical project, even though it employs sceptical arguments along the way.

You may well be familiar with the indubitable fixed-point that Descartes claimed that he discovered using this sceptical methodology, since this is where his famous remark '*cogito ergo sum*' comes in (known as *the cogito*, for short). This is usually translated, albeit not without some controversy, as 'I think, therefore I am'. In a nutshell, Descartes's idea was that while one can doubt most of what one believes—we will consider just why he claimed this in a moment—one cannot doubt one's own existence. After all, in doubting it, one is thereby thinking, and that means that one must be in existence in order to be doing the thinking in the first place. That one exists is thus meant to be an indubitable, and hence epistemically secure, foundation for our knowledge.

More specifically, what Descartes was seeking as a foundation for knowledge was certainty, and that the *cogito* is indubitable is meant to show that it is something the truth of which we can be certain of.

Interestingly, while Descartes's brand of foundationalism has not proved to be popular, the radical scepticism that he set out in order to motivate this style of foundationalism continues to grip the philosophical imagination. Part of the reason for this is that there are some fairly serious difficulties that afflict the particular foundationalist account that Descartes goes on to develop, not least in terms of how it essentially appeals to God's existence (and also to God's epistemically benevolent nature). But another part of the reason for the enduring appeal of Descartes's formulation of radical scepticism concerns its employment of an important theoretical innovation that is these days known as a *radical sceptical hypothesis*.

A radical sceptical hypothesis is a possibility of error that has two key features. The first is that it is a scenario that is completely indistinguishable from one's everyday life. The second is that it is a scenario in which most of what one believes is false. These two features make radical sceptical hypotheses very different from the kinds of possibilities of error that one usually encounters. Consider the mundane error-possibility, noted in Chapter 1, that one's car, which one believes to be parked outside, has in fact been stolen. There is nothing indistinguishable about this scenario, as one only needs to go outside one's house to verify whether it is true. Moreover, although it calls some of one's beliefs into question—most specifically one's belief about the current location of one's car—it doesn't call one's beliefs as a whole into question at all. Radical sceptical hypotheses are thus very different to everyday error-possibilities.

Descartes presents two very vivid radical sceptical hypotheses in his *Meditations*. The first is the possibility that one is experiencing a particularly realistic dream. Dreams can be very credible, even to the point that one can be convinced that one is wide awake. It thus seems at least possible that what one is experiencing right now could be just a dream—that is, that it is one of those hyper-real dreams that seem so real that one doesn't realize that one is dreaming. If one were in such a dream, then it would be completely indistinguishable from normal waking life. For example, there would be no point pinching oneself to make sure that one is awake, since if one is in the dream then the pinching would simply form part of the dream-like state itself.

If one were in the grip of such a dream, then although one would seem to be experiencing the world around one (the 'external world') in the usual way, in fact one's sensory experiences would not be hooked-up to the external world at all. Instead, they would be the product of one's imagination. Given that one's apparent sensory experiences in one's dreams are the result of one's imagination rather than the external world, one can see how they might end up generating mostly false beliefs about the external world. It could be, for example, that none of what you take yourself to have experienced in the past really happened, and that you only believed that it happened because of what you experienced in the dream. In that case, all your beliefs about these events could be false. (As the Chinese philosopher Zhuang Zhou (*c.369–c.286* BCE) posed it, many years before Descartes, how is one to know that one is a human being who is dreaming that one is a butterfly as opposed to being a butterfly who is dreaming that one is a human being?)

We now have an error-possibility that is indistinguishable from everyday life but where most of one's beliefs are false (since one's beliefs about the external world comprise a large component of your beliefs as a whole). We thus have a *radical sceptical hypothesis*. Note too what this radical sceptical hypothesis is calling into question, which is the truth of one's beliefs about the external world. This is why Cartesian scepticism is sometimes called external world scepticism.

As just noted, we are all familiar with dreams, and how they might deceive us. For Descartes, however, the dreaming radical sceptical hypothesis is meant to just soften us up for an even more extreme, and supernatural, error-possibility. This is the possibility that there is a malevolent demon who has the power, and inclination, to systematically deceive us, albeit in a way that is completely hidden from us. We know that our senses are fallible, so why couldn't it be possible for there to be a creature who is able to ensure that our sensory experience is always misleading, but without this ever being detectable, even in principle? Perhaps, for example, they can generate within us the sensory experience of walking in a forest when we are in fact floating on water; or can make us believe that we are high up on a mountain when in fact we are deep in a dark cave. While incredible, the point is that this scenario does not seem at all impossible. But with this degree of deception in play there wouldn't be any way in which we could distinguish these misleading experiences from the genuine article. Moreover, most of our beliefs formed on the basis of these deceptive experiences would tend to be false—for example, one would believe that one is on top of a mountain when one is in fact inside a cave.

Thus far, the 'evil demon' error-possibility is much like the dream scenario in that both are calling the general veracity of our sensory experiences into question, and hence prompting us to doubt the truth of our beliefs about the external world. The two sceptical scenarios diverge in terms of the scope of the beliefs that they call into question, however. In particular, with the evil demon sceptical hypothesis one seems able to not just make one's sensory experiences unreliable, but also (just about) *any* belief-forming process that one cares to imagine.

For example, one might naturally suppose that one's confidence in simple arithmetical truths, such as that '4 + 4 = 8', is immune to the dreaming sceptical hypothesis. After all, couldn't one do these sums even in one's dreams, and thereby end up with a true mathematical belief even if all of one's sensory beliefs were false? Crucially, however, the evil demon could surely interfere with your mental processes just as they interfere with your sensory experiences. In this way, they could make it feel like you are undertaking elementary arithmetical calculations with obviously true conclusions when in fact you are fundamentally in error. Under the influence of such an evil demon, couldn't one form the belief that '4 + 4 = 2' with just as much conviction as one would form the belief that '4 + 4 = 8' in ordinary circumstances? If so, then nearly all of one's beliefs could be undetectably false, where this means not just one's beliefs about the external world formed on the basis of apparent sensory experiences, but also one's beliefs formed in non-sensory ways, even those that are the result of apparently impeccable rational processes like basic arithmetic.

The evil demon error-possibility is thus an even more radical sceptical hypothesis than the dreaming hypothesis in that it doesn't just call the truth of one's beliefs in an external world into question, but also the truth of one's beliefs that aren't about such an external world. Indeed, the only belief whose truth is not called into question by the evil demon radical sceptical hypothesis seems to be the *cogito*, which shows just how extensive the sceptical scope of this error-possibility is.

Are you a brain in a vat?

Descartes's 17th-century audience clearly had no problem taking the idea of such a mischievous demon seriously. In our more secular and scientific time, however, I imagine that many would find this intellectual device perhaps a bit too fantastical. But this really doesn't matter because we can easily come up with error-possibilities that have exactly the same kinds of scepticism-inducing properties without having to resort to such supernatural entities. Indeed, as we will see, all we need to do is go to the cinema.

So, for example, here is a contemporary variation on the evil demon radical sceptical hypothesis that you might be familiar with (in some form or other) from Hollywood movies such as *The Matrix*. Let's imagine that there are evil scientists who go about 'harvesting' brains from bodies and keeping those brains alive in vats of nutrients where they are 'fed' experiences by supercomputers. Crucially, the experiences that these 'brains in a vat', or *BIVs* for short, are given are indistinguishable from one's everyday experiences (Figure 5). In addition, the BIVs have no memories of being abducted and put in the vats. This means that the BIVs are completely unaware that they are now living their lives entirely within the fake virtual environment created by the supercomputers. So, for example, the BIVs have experiences as if they are walking around in their normal environment, interacting with friends and colleagues, driving their cars to the shops, and so on. And yet none of this is actually happening, since all of these experiences are in fact manufactured by the machines plugged into the vat. Accordingly, most of what our BIVs believe is false, and hence they don't know very much, if anything. They are being systematically deceived, but not by a supernatural being as Descartes envisaged, but rather by the evil scientists in charge of the technology that they are embedded in.

Notice how similar the BIV radical sceptical hypothesis is to Descartes's evil demon scenario. Since the supercomputers are generating fake sensory experiences, they are blocking off our sensory access to the external world. But it isn't just our sensory experiences that they are fabricating, since they can fabricate *any* of our experiences at will. Accordingly, just like the evil demon, they can make me believe that I have just conducted an impeccable chain of reasoning, such as an elementary piece of arithmetic, even when I've done nothing of the sort. We thus get a sceptical scenario not only suitable for the kind of external world scepticism that is distinctively Cartesian, but also one that can call the truth of even our beliefs that aren't concerned with the external world into question.

5. The brain in a vat. We think we are embodied people interacting within a shared social world, but could we instead be nothing more than disembodied brains floating in a vat of nutrients, being 'fed' our experiences by supercomputers?

Now all this talk of BIVs is all very science fiction, of course. But note that no-one is saying that this scenario is true, or even likely (just as Descartes wasn't claiming that there really is an evil demon that is deceiving you). Right now, the sceptic is merely noting that this hypothesis is *possible*—that is, it is something that

31

could happen, no matter how unlikely it might be. And that is certainly true. After all, the scenario as described does not depict anything impossible occurring, and so we ought to concede that it is entirely possible.

Moreover, even if there were something about this scenario that might make us think that it is impossible, then we could just come up with a different radical sceptical scenario. Since the BIV scenario is found in the movies, let's pick another radical sceptical hypothesis that we find in a Hollywood film. This time consider the scenario as depicted in the film *Inception* (Figure 6). This depicts fully-coherent dream-like states that people can inhabit in which everything seems completely normal, when in fact nothing that one is apparently experiencing is actually happening. As we noted with regard to Descartes's sceptical dream hypothesis above, it does seem at least possible that all of your experiences right now could be the product of a dream-like state. If that were so, however, then most of what you believe would be false. You are not in fact sitting at a coffee shop drinking a coffee with your

6. Scepticism at the movies. Many movies, such as *Inception* pictured here, make use of radical sceptical hypotheses as a dramatic device.

friends right now, you didn't visit your parents yesterday, and you won't actually be driving to the coast for the day with your children tomorrow either—everything is rather just a part of the dream-like state that you are presently inhabiting.

Or, since we are taking our cue from the movies, how about the radical sceptical scenario involved in the film *The Truman Show*? This concerns someone who thinks he is leading a normal life, but who is in fact the lead character in a TV show. Accordingly, everyone around him is an actor, and the environment in which he interacts with others is nothing more than a TV set. As before, our hero's experiences on the TV set are indistinguishable from experiences one might have in everyday life, where one is genuinely living a normal life rather than having the whole thing staged for one in a TV studio. Moreover, a great deal of what he believes is false. He doesn't live in a normal town, his friends are not his friends but actors pretending to be his friends, the shops he goes to are not real shops but sound stages, and so on. And since a lot of what he believes is false, it also follows that he doesn't know a lot of what he takes himself to know either.

(Notice that this sceptical scenario is a little different from the dream-like hypothesis depicted in *Inception*, where one's experiences aren't hooked-up to the external world at all. Instead, although the protagonist in *The Truman Show* is genuinely interacting with an external world, he fundamentally misunderstands the nature of this interaction. In both cases the upshot is the same in that our deceived subject knows much less about the external world than they imagine.)

The point is that once we understand how radical sceptical hypotheses are set up, then it is fairly straightforward to come up with new ones. There is thus very little to be gained by objecting to the sceptic's claim that such scenarios are at least possible. In any case, on the face of it, to concede this is not to concede very much anyway. After all, although it is clear that the BIV, as with

33

other victims of radical sceptical hypotheses, has lots of false beliefs, and hence doesn't know very much, why should that have any relevance for us? Remember that the sceptic hasn't claimed that we are BIVs (or the victim of any other radical sceptical hypothesis for that matter). Indeed, they haven't even claimed that such scenarios are likely, so for all that's been said so far we can treat them as completely far-fetched error-possibilities (which is what they seem to be). As a result, why should the fact that the BIV doesn't know very much have any bearing on what we know?

The sceptic now makes an important move, which is to point out that it is *impossible to rule out* a radical sceptical hypothesis. That is, it seems that one cannot know that one is not the victim of a radical sceptical hypothesis. One cannot know, for instance, that one is not a BIV. For how would one go about knowing that one is not a BIV, given that the experiences had by the BIV are indistinguishable from one's everyday experiences? For example, it would clearly be pointless to note that you can see and feel your body right now, and hence conclude that you can't be a bodiless BIV, since of course the BIV also has the same experiences you do as if they have a body (albeit misleading experiences in their case). Equally, there would be no point in grabbing objects in one's environment—picking up a cup on one's desk, for example—and concluding that one can't be a BIV since BIVs don't physically engage with their environment. This is because, as before, BIVs will have experiences just like you do as if they are engaging with objects in their environment, even though in fact they are doing nothing of the kind.

Interestingly, it would also be similarly pointless to respond to the BIV sceptical scenario by arguing that one has scientific grounds for thinking that there are no BIVs at present. In particular, one might be tempted to argue that since the current state of technology is not advanced enough for there to be BIVs, hence we have a rational basis for ruling out this sceptical scenario. A moment's reflection reveals that considerations like this have no bearing at all on the issue in hand. After all, one's envatted counterpart could be being 'fed' similar information regarding the current state of technological development and so will draw exactly the same conclusion, even though in their case that conclusion would be false. Accordingly, that one believes that our current science couldn't support BIVs is neither here nor there when it comes to evaluating this sceptical scenario.

The upshot is that since radical sceptical hypotheses like the BIV scenario are indistinguishable from everyday experiences, it follows that we cannot rule them out. And that in turn means that we are unable to know that we are not the victims of such scenarios. Put another way, for all we know, we could be BIVs (or in the grip of a hyper-real dream, or being deceived by an evil demon, and so on).

So the sceptic has now made two moves. The first has been to describe what a radical sceptical hypothesis is, and to argue that such hypotheses depict possible scenarios. The second has been to argue that we cannot rule out these radical sceptical hypotheses, and hence that we do not know that they are false.

Has the sceptic done enough to motivate their sceptical conclusion that we don't know much of what we take ourselves to know (such as regarding the external world)? If one held that knowledge demands that one is infallible or completely certain, then this would be a plausible conclusion to draw. After all, the sceptic has alerted us to a class of error-possibilities that we cannot rule out, error-possibilities that call into question the truth of much of what we believe. Clearly, then, we cannot credibly regard our everyday knowledge as being infallible, since we have just described a sceptical scenario in which we would believe exactly what we do now but believe falsely (e.g. if one actually were a BIV). Moreover, since we know that we cannot rule out these radical sceptical error-possibilities, then how can we be absolutely certain that what we ordinarily believe is true? Relatedly, if one is engaged in the epistemological enterprise of seeking a foundation for knowledge that is indubitable, and hence absolutely certain, as Descartes was, then one is not going to hold that one's everyday beliefs could ever fulfil that role.

But as we saw in Chapter 1, however, it doesn't seem at all credible that the bar for knowledge should be set so high as to demand infallibility or absolute certainty (or, for that matter, indubitability). On the contrary, our everyday conception of knowledge seems to leave us perfectly happy with the idea that knowledge can be fallible and not absolutely certain (and thus to a degree dubitable) while being bona fide knowledge nonetheless. What matters is that we have good epistemic reasons for believing what we do, and we can have such reasons even in the absence of infallibility and absolutely certainty. If that's right, then insisting that knowledge is lacking would be akin to illicitly changing the subject. The sceptic would in effect be arguing that we lack knowledge relative to a specific, and highly demanding, account of 'knowledge' that is radically distinct from how we in fact use the notion of knowledge in everyday discourse. But why should we care about that? To use an analogy that a contemporary philosopher has offered, it would be like coming across someone who claims that there are no doctors in New York City on the grounds that by 'doctor' they mean someone who can cure any disease within twenty-four hours. No-one would be impressed by 'doctor' scepticism of this kind. Why should radical scepticism about knowledge be any different?

The crux of the matter is that the mere fact that there are these radical sceptical hypotheses involving massive error that we cannot rule out doesn't itself show that there is anything epistemically amiss with our everyday knowledge. At most, it reminds us that such knowledge is fallible, and hence that we shouldn't be absolutely certain of what we believe. But we knew that already. As we noted, the mere possibility of error does not suffice to undermine knowledge provided that this possibility is remote. And for all the radical sceptic has said otherwise, these radical sceptical hypotheses are depicting remote possibilities of error. For remember that the sceptic has not claimed that the radical sceptical hypotheses they propose are likely, or even that they are true. So what is to stop us from treating them as the far-fetched error-possibilities that they appear to be? If that's right, then there seems nothing amiss with supposing that we know most of what we take ourselves to know. It is just that there are some error-possibilities—those picked out by radical sceptical hypotheses—that we cannot know to be false.

Unfortunately, as we will now see, the radical sceptic is only just getting warmed up. In particular, there is a way of supplementing the radical sceptical hypotheses with a further very credible principle in order to serve the sceptic's ends. In particular, this allows the radical sceptic to motivate their sceptical conclusion without having to appeal to the idea that knowledge demands infallibility or absolute certainty.

Scepticism and closure

Here is the state of play. The radical sceptic has argued that we cannot know that we are not victims of radical sceptical hypotheses, like the BIV scenario. But on the face of it that seems entirely compatible with the idea that we know much of what we take ourselves to know—that I know where I live, what I ate for breakfast today, what jersey I'm currently wearing, and so on (which are all things, by the way, that the BIV doesn't know). So how can the radical sceptic use the claim that we can't rule out radical sceptical hypotheses to motivate their sceptical doubt?

This is where the radical sceptic introduces a principle that at first blush can seem entirely innocuous, but which, as we will see, greatly strengthens their hand. Consider the following reasoning. Suppose you know that the name of the capital of France begins with the letter 'P'. Then aren't you also in a position to know that

Madrid is not the capital of France (since 'Madrid' doesn't begin with the letter 'P')? Or take another example. Suppose you know that the single most populous country on the planet is China. Then aren't you also in a position to know that India is not the most populous country on the planet (given that there can be only one country that is the single most populous country on the planet)?

The reasoning at issue here looks harmless, and that's precisely because the inferences in play are so obvious, given what you know. What such inferences illustrate is that if you know one proposition (e.g. that the capital of France begins with the letter 'P'; or that China is the single most populous country on the planet), and you know that this proposition entails a second proposition (e.g. that Madrid is not the capital of France; or that India is not the single most populous country on the planet), then you know that second proposition too. What could be more innocuous than that?

The principle at issue here is the idea that knowledge is preserved, or 'closed', under known entailment. This is why it is often called *the closure principle* for short. It is hard to see how such a principle could possibly fail. How could it be that one knows one proposition, knows that this entails a second proposition, and yet fail to know that second proposition? After all, precisely what it means for one proposition to entail another is that if the entailing proposition is true, then the entailed proposition must be true also. So if it is true that China is the single most populous country on the planet, then it must also be true that India is not the single most populous country on the planet. But if you know that something is true, and know that if this is true then something else must be true, then how could you fail to know that this second claim is true as well? For example, how could one know that China is the single most populous country on the planet, and know that if China is the single most populous country on the planet then India is not the single most populous country on the planet, and yet fail to know that India is not the single most populous country on the planet?

(Indeed, imagine someone who claimed to know both that China is the single most populous country on the planet and that this entails that India is not the single most populous country on the planet, but who nonetheless maintained that they didn't know that India is not the single most populous country on the planet. Does this even make sense? Wouldn't we think that they must be confused in some way, such as that they don't really understand what they are claiming?)

The closure principle thus looks very compelling. The problem, however, is that the radical sceptic can employ this seemingly harmless principle to motivate their radical sceptical doubt. For notice that just about any everyday claim that you take yourself to know is going to be inconsistent with some radical sceptical hypothesis or other. For example, right now I take myself to know that I am wearing a shirt. I can see that I am wearing a shirt, I can feel it on my skin, I remember putting it on this morning, other people can tell me that I am wearing a shirt, and so on. There is thus an abundance of evidence that I am wearing a shirt. But if it is true that I am wearing a shirt, then it is also true that I am not a BIV. After all, BIVs don't have bodies, and so they can't wear shirts. Thus it can't both be true that I am wearing a shirt and that I am a BIV. Put another way, that I am wearing a shirt entails that I am not a BIV.

The difficulties start, however, once we begin to plug this entailment into a closure-style inference. For suppose I do know that I am wearing a shirt. We've just noted that I also know that wearing a shirt entails that I am not a BIV. But we have also agreed with the sceptic that I cannot rule out the BIV sceptical hypothesis, and hence do not know that I'm not a BIV. Accordingly, it seems that I know that I'm wearing a shirt, know that if I'm wearing a shirt then I'm not a BIV, but I don't know that I'm not a BIV. And that sounds entirely wrong. How can I know that I'm wearing a shirt, but not whether I'm a shirtless BIV? Given the plausibility of the closure principle, it thus seems that if I did know that I'm wearing a shirt, then I must be able to know that I'm not a BIV. Conversely, if it really is impossible to know that I'm not a BIV, then it must also be impossible to know that I'm wearing a shirt. With the closure principle in play, then, the radical sceptic can thus use our inability to rule out radical sceptical hypotheses to undermine our everyday knowledge, such as one's seemingly uncontentious knowledge that one is wearing a shirt.

And notice that what goes here for knowing that one is wearing a shirt applies to one's knowledge of a myriad range of everyday claims. For example, knowing that one is driving one's car or that one is playing the violin are both inconsistent with being a BIV, and hence one could run exactly the same reasoning to show that such 'knowledge' is completely illusory. Moreover, as we noted above, the BIV radical sceptical hypothesis is but one sceptical scenario, as we can easily cook up other radical sceptical hypotheses. There is thus nothing stopping the radical sceptic from using the closure principle to motivate sceptical doubt of a wide range of everyday claims that we think we know.

You should now be starting to see the shape of the puzzle. Prior to considering the closure principle, it seemed that one could grant that one is unable to know the denials of radical sceptical hypotheses without this having any implications for scepticism. This was because one's knowledge of everyday claims seemed to be unaffected by one's inability to rule out such fantastical scenarios. But once we realize that our everyday beliefs are in conflict with radical sceptical hypotheses, such that the truth of the former entails the falsity of the latter, then this situation ceases to be stable. If we really do know the everyday claims that we take ourselves to know (e.g. that one is wearing a shirt), then, incredibly, it seems we must be able to know the denials of radical sceptical hypotheses after all (e.g. that one is not a BIV). Alternatively, insofar as the sceptic is right that we are unable to know the denials of radical sceptical hypotheses, then it seems we must also be unable to know these everyday claims as well. That is, if I really don't know that I'm not a BIV, then I can't know that I'm wearing a shirt, and any other everyday claim that is inconsistent with a radical sceptical hypothesis. With the closure principle in play, therefore, the sceptic seems able to motivate a radical sceptical doubt.

In fact, once we reflect on the matter, this sceptical conclusion ought not to be that surprising. We have noted that knowledge is true belief that is grounded in good epistemic reasons. My putative knowledge that I am wearing a shirt is, so I thought, grounded in such good epistemic reasons as that I can see the shirt, I can remember putting it on, I can feel it on my torso, and so on. But if I am a BIV, then I would seem to have all the same epistemic reasons and yet my belief that I am wearing a shirt would be false. Indeed, this is precisely the reason why I can't know that I'm not a BIV in that I have no good epistemic reasons for thinking that this is the case (on account of the fact that the BIV's experiences are indistinguishable from normal experiences). So how then can I have good epistemic reasons for believing that I am presently wearing a shirt, and yet have no good epistemic reasons for believing that I am not a (shirtless) BIV? The sceptical point is clear: insofar as you really have no good epistemic reasons for believing that you are not a (shirtless) BIV, then you don't really have any good epistemic reasons for believing that you are wearing a shirt either. What you have are merely *apparently* good epistemic reasons for believing everyday claims such as that you are wearing a shirt, but since they are not reasons that distinguish between the everyday scenario (wearing a shirt) and the incompatible sceptical scenario (being a shirtless BIV), they cannot be *genuinely* good epistemic reasons at all. In short, while you might think that you have good epistemic reasons for believing many of the things that you believe, in fact you don't have any good reasons for believing these things at all. And that's why you don't know many of the everyday claims that you take yourself to know.

This highlights an important point about radical scepticism of this kind. The sceptical claim is not merely that one does not know many of the things that one takes oneself to know. Rather, it is the stronger thesis that one does not have any good epistemic reason for believing many of the things that one takes oneself to know. The former claim is compatible with one having *some* good epistemic reasons for believing what one does, but where these reasons are insufficient for knowledge. The radical sceptical contention in play is, however, much more dramatic: that one has no good epistemic reason at all for believing even such apparently mundane everyday claims as that one is presently wearing a shirt. Accordingly, if your beliefs in this regard happen to be true, then that is just a matter of luck from an epistemic point of view, just like it's purely a matter of luck that the gullible person who believes anything they are told might end up with some true beliefs.

The upshot is that it seems that if we want to have good epistemic reasons for believing the everyday things that we take ourselves to know, then we need to be able to rule out radical sceptical hypotheses. And since we cannot do the latter, it follows that we don't have good epistemic reasons for much of what we believe, and hence we can't know what we believe either. By employing the closure principle the radical sceptic appears to have been able to turn the apparently harmless claim that we can't rule out radical sceptical scenarios into something with important sceptical consequences. Even though the sceptic has offered us no reasons for thinking that the radical sceptical hypotheses are true, or even likely, they are still able to use these scenarios to extract radical sceptical conclusions. Note too that there is no appeal to infallibility (or complete certainty) going on here. If the radical sceptic is right that we don't have any epistemic reasons at all in support of our everyday beliefs, then it follows that we lack even fallible (or somewhat uncertain) knowledge of these everyday claims.

The radical sceptical paradox

We are now in a position to put all the moving parts of this formulation of radical scepticism together. In essence, the radical sceptic maintains that the following three claims are *inconsistent*, which means that they cannot all be true (i.e. at least one of them must be false):

(1) We are unable to know the denials of radical sceptical hypotheses.
(2) The closure principle.
(3) We have lots of knowledge of everyday claims.

We have seen that (1) is eminently plausible. This is because radical sceptical hypotheses are precisely characterized in such a way that they are indistinguishable from normal life. Life in the vat for the BIV is exactly like a normal life out of the vat, even though most of the BIV's beliefs are false. (2) is also very plausible. Surely, as the closure principle demands, if one knows one proposition, and knows that it entails a second proposition, then one must know the second proposition? But, as we have seen, with (1) and (2) in play it seems that (3) becomes unsustainable. For if we did know these everyday claims (such as that one is wearing a shirt), then given that we know that they are inconsistent with radical sceptical hypotheses (e.g. that one is a BIV), it would seem to follow, via the closure principle, that we must be able to know the denials of radical sceptical hypotheses. But given that we cannot know the denials of radical sceptical hypotheses, it follows that we don't know the everyday claims either. And yet we do ordinarily suppose that we have lots of everyday knowledge, in line with (3). Indeed, as we noted above, it seems that our inability to know the denials of radical sceptical hypotheses means that we have no good epistemic reasons at all for our everyday beliefs. Thus, we can't consistently endorse all three of (1), (2), and (3).

I have deliberately expressed the sceptical challenge as an inconstant set of claims in order to highlight two distinct ways of characterizing the problem of radical scepticism. We can think of radical scepticism as either being a *position*, or as merely posing a *paradox*. So, for example, radical scepticism understood as a position would respond to the inconsistent set of claims just listed and conclude that since (1) and (2) are clearly true, hence it should be (3) that we reject. In particular, radical scepticism as a position would conclude that from (1) and (2) it follows that we do not have much of the everyday knowledge that we take ourselves to have, and hence that (3) is false.

Interestingly, however, the radical sceptic doesn't need to go this far in order to intellectually disquiet us. It is enough, after all, to notice that we seem to be independently committed to each of (1), (2), and (3), and yet they can't all be true. That is, all three of these claims appear to be rooted in our ordinary way of thinking about knowledge, which is why we find each of these claims so compelling. But there must be something amiss with our ordinary conception of knowledge if it leads to inconsistent claims in this fashion.

This way of characterizing the problem of radical scepticism conceives it as a paradox rather than a position. On this rendering, the radical sceptic doesn't tell us which of the three claims that we should give up, but only that we are committed to all three of them even though they can't all be true. There is a rich history in philosophy of posing paradoxes of this kind. That is, in thinking hard about our most fundamental everyday concepts—time, freedom, causation, and so on—and showing that they seem to generate inconsistent claims.

There are advantages to proposing the radical sceptical challenge in terms of a paradox rather than a position. If one opts for the latter strategy, after all, then it is open to us to query the coherence of this stance. We might ask the radical sceptic who denies (3), for example, how they are meant to live their lives. How plausible is it that one can go about their daily existence without supposing that one knows a great deal? As we noted at the end of Chapter 1, it is hard to even make sense of the idea that one can live one's life completely deprived of knowledge without one's existence becoming absurd as a result. At the very least, the radical sceptic seems to owe us an explanation of how living the radically sceptical life is even feasible.

If one proposes radical scepticism as a paradox, however, then one is under no such obligation to explain oneself. After all, the paradox is simply composed of claims that we all seem compelled to accept. The tension is thus arising exclusively out of our own commitments. The onus is therefore on ourselves to work out how we are going to resolve this inconsistency in our thinking about knowledge, preferably in such a way that avoids the sceptical option of rejecting (3).

In any case, notice that this sceptical challenge, whether formulated as a paradox or as a position, satisfies the *desiderata* that we previously laid down for sceptical doubt. In particular, there is no appeal to infallibility or complete certainty in this argument, but only to our regular, fallible, conception of knowledge. Relatedly, it is not the mere possibility of error that is generating the sceptical doubt, but rather the combination of this possibility of error and the closure principle. It is the latter that is ensuring that the radical sceptical hypotheses, while apparently remote error-possibilities, are nonetheless relevant to determining whether we have knowledge of everyday claims. This is because of how we are aware that those everyday claims are inconsistent with radical sceptical hypotheses. It is also worth reminding ourselves that the sceptic is not claiming that these radical sceptical hypotheses are true (e.g. they are not claiming that we are BIVs), or even that we have any rational basis for thinking that such hypotheses are likely. Given the closure principle, just so long as these scenarios are possible and we are unable to rule them out (i.e. know them to be false), then their inconsistency with our everyday beliefs will be enough to motivate the radical sceptical challenge.

We thus seem to have a genuine radical sceptical argument on our hands. It is an argument that purports to call our widespread knowledge of the world around us into question. In particular, the argument isn't directed at the truth of our beliefs, but rather at the epistemic grounds that we have for those beliefs, even if true. Since, as we noted above, there is more to knowledge than mere true belief in that knowledge additionally demands epistemic grounds for one's true belief, it follows that so long as the sceptic can undermine these grounds for belief then they can thereby undermine our knowledge. Indeed, if this radical sceptical argument works, then we not only lack knowledge of much of what we believe, but we don't even have any good epistemic reasons for believing what we do.

In Chapter 3 we will consider some responses to this formulation of radical scepticism.

Chapter 3
Defending knowledge

Let's remind ourselves of the radical sceptical puzzle that we set out in Chapter 2. Recall that it involved showing that the following three claims are all independently plausible, but can't all be true (i.e. at least one of them must be false):

(1) We are unable to know the denials of radical sceptical hypotheses.
(2) The closure principle.
(3) We have lots of knowledge of everyday claims.

(1) is plausible because radical sceptical hypotheses are precisely characterized in such a way that they are indistinguishable from normal life. As to (2), recall that the closure principle is the compelling claim that if one knows one proposition, and knows that it entails a second proposition, then one also knows the second proposition. So (2) looks secure too. And we naturally want to maintain (3). The problem is, however, that with (1) and (2) in play it seems that (3) becomes unsustainable. For if we did know these everyday claims (e.g. that one is wearing a shirt), then given that we know that they are inconsistent with radical sceptical hypotheses (e.g. that one is a BIV), it would seem to follow, via the closure principle, that we must be able to know the denials of radical sceptical hypotheses. But given that we cannot know the denials of radical sceptical hypotheses, it follows that we don't know the everyday claims either. Indeed, as we noted above,

47

it seems that our inability to know the denials of radical sceptical hypotheses means that we have no good epistemic reasons at all for our everyday beliefs. Thus, we can't consistently endorse all three of (1), (2), and (3).

The danger, of course, is that the radical sceptic will convince us that the best way of responding to this difficulty is to endorse (1) and (2), and thereby reject (3). The result would be a radical sceptical doubt regarding much of what we hitherto took ourselves to know. But even if we don't conclude that (3) should be rejected, and thus endorse radical scepticism as a position, there is still a puzzle here. How can we be independently committed to these three claims that are jointly inconsistent? This is the *paradox* of radical scepticism (as distinct from radical scepticism as a *position*). And it is no less of a reason to doubt that we know much of what we take ourselves to know.

In this chapter we are going to be considering some responses to this puzzle.

Scepticism and commonsense

Let's start with a very natural response to philosophical puzzles like this, which is to insist on our commonsense principles and work back from there. In short, if radical scepticism conflicts with commonsense—and surely it does—then isn't that a sound basis for dismissing radical scepticism?

That's certainly a very reasonable place to start in our dealings with radical scepticism, since what could be more reasonable than commonsense? Indeed, the idea that commonsense should be theoretically privileged in this way also has a decent philosophical pedigree in that it has been endorsed in various forms by prominent philosophers over the years, including Thomas Reid (1710–96) and G. E. Moore (1873–1958). One of the difficulties facing this approach to radical scepticism, however, is that the sceptical puzzle that we are engaging with doesn't seem to rest on anything *but* commonsense. That is, the three claims that we have noted as being inconsistent above all appear to arise out of our ordinary ways of thinking about knowledge. For example, as we noted in Chapter 2, none of these claims obviously presupposes contentious ideas about knowledge such as that it is infallible or demands complete certainty. If that's right, then it seems that it is commonsense itself that is generating the sceptical puzzle, by virtue of the fact that our own commonsense conception of knowledge leads to contradiction.

Now one might counter this by noting that although the inconsistent claims (1) to (3) that make up our puzzle are all individually compelling, they nonetheless do appeal to notions that we don't ordinarily find in our everyday practices. In particular, we do not normally even consider radical sceptical hypotheses in our day-to-day life. With that in mind, could we use an appeal to commonsense to coherently argue that the esoteric nature of radical sceptical scenarios means that we shouldn't have to rule them out in order to have widespread everyday knowledge?

There are a number of difficulties with this suggestion. To begin with, it is far from clear that radical sceptical hypotheses really are that esoteric. After all, as we noted previously, such scenarios are a mainstay of Hollywood movies, including some blockbusters, so how plausible is it that they are somehow at odds with commonsense thinking? Aren't they in fact rather familiar possibilities of error?

But even if such scenarios really were as arcane as this proposal suggests, that wouldn't by itself demonstrate that radical sceptical scenarios are contrary to commonsense ways of thinking. In order to see this point we need to remind ourselves that in everyday life we are often constrained in lots of incidental ways. For example, when evaluating whether a belief amounts to knowledge we simply might not have the time to consider whether all the relevant possibilities of error have been excluded, or may even lack the imagination to come up with the full list anyway. Moreover, our everyday practices of evaluating knowledge will inevitably involve some short cuts and rules-of-thumb, as we navigate ourselves around the practical hurdles that face us in day-to-day life.

Crucially, however, when we do philosophy it is usually important to set aside these purely practical constraints, since they are normally irrelevant. This is especially so in the field of philosophy that concerns us, which is *epistemology* (i.e. the area of philosophy devoted to questions about truth, knowledge, and related notions). Suppose, for example, that it turned out that when we consider, as epistemologists, the basis for a particular knowledge claim we discover that in fact it is very shaky due to the fact that there is a relevant possibility of error that most people in everyday life are simply unaware of and hence don't consider. (As it happens, this is not a merely theoretical possibility, as cognitive scientists have demonstrated that there are a whole range of cognitive biases that influence our reasoning, often negatively, of which we are often completely unaware.) Would we conclude from the fact that in everyday life we don't consider this possibility of error that therefore we *shouldn't* consider it, and hence that the knowledge claim in question is entirely secure? Surely not. Instead we would argue that while in fact we don't consider this possibility of error, we *ought* to.

The point is that even if we don't in fact consider radical sceptical hypotheses in our day-to-day lives, that doesn't by itself suffice to demonstrate that we ought not to. In any case, even if we granted that there was something problematic about our consideration of radical sceptical hypotheses from a commonsense perspective, it isn't obvious how this would help us resolve the problem of radical scepticism anyway. After all, the closure principle is surely rooted in our commonsense thinking about knowledge. But if that's right, then it seems to follow that we can only have knowledge of everyday claims where we are also able to know whatever is entailed by these everyday claims. For if it turns out that we can't know the latter, then, via closure, it will follow that we can't know the former either. So, for example, if I can't know that I am not presently shirtless, then I can't know that I'm presently wearing a shirt, since of course wearing a shirt entails that one is not shirtless. Knowing that one is presently wearing a shirt thus demands, given closure, that one can know that one is not presently shirtless.

We have just stated this implication of the closure principle without mentioning radical sceptical hypotheses, so nothing we've expressed so far ought to be problematic from the perspective of commonsense. But whether we mention radical sceptical hypotheses or not, it ought to be clear that this implication of the closure principle will just as much apply to these scenarios. After all, one way that I could be shirtless is to be a BIV who lacks a body to put a shirt on. So if in order to know that I am presently wearing a shirt I need to be able to rule out scenarios where I am shirtless, then that means I need to be able to rule out the BIV radical sceptical scenario. It follows that regardless of whether one explicitly mentions radical sceptical hypotheses, that one needs to rule them out in order to have everyday knowledge does seem to be a consequence of our commonsense ways of thinking about knowledge.

Simply appealing to commonsense thus doesn't seem to offer much that is tangible when it comes to responding to the sceptical puzzle. A more subtle way of employing commonsense in this regard was famously offered by G. E. Moore, writing almost a century ago. His idea was that when philosophy and commonsense conflict, then we are entitled to push back against philosophy by appealing to commonsense. To use a famous example that he offered in this regard, in normal circumstances nothing is more certain than that one has hands (Figure 7). It is thus the kind of claim that is core to our commonsense picture of the world. Accordingly, if philosophy tells us that we don't know that we have

7. Hands. G. E. Moore famously thought that there was nothing more certain, in normal conditions, than that one has two hands, though what import this has for the problem of scepticism is moot. (This detail is from Jan Cornelisz Vermeyen's 'Portrait of Erard de la Marck', *c.*1530.)

hands, and hence conflicts with commonsense, then so much the worse for philosophy. How would this idea play out with regard to the radical sceptical puzzle in hand?

Here is Moore's proposal, in outline. From a commonsense perspective, the idea that we have lots of everyday knowledge, encapsulated in (3), is clearly sacrosanct, as giving up on that would be a disaster. For one thing, it would mean giving up on our knowledge that we have hands. The closure principle, and hence (2), also looks very secure. So given that we need to reject at least one of the claims (1) to (3), how about we embrace (3) and (2) and hence conclude that (1) must be false? Scepticism as a position, recall, advocates accepting that we can't know the denials of radical sceptical hypotheses (1), and hence concluding, via the closure principle (2), that we don't know much of what we ordinarily take ourselves to know (i.e. they conclude that (3) is false). But Moore's suggestion is to use this reasoning in reverse.

That is, we should embrace the idea that we do know the everyday things that we take ourselves to know (3), and hence, via the closure principle (2), we should conclude that we do know the denials of radical sceptical hypotheses after all (i.e. we should reject (1)).

In proposing this, Moore grants two crucial points to the radical sceptic. The first is that the sceptic's reasoning is just as good as our reasoning. That is, he isn't arguing that the radical sceptic's way of denying (3) is wrong. He is just saying that we can equally argue in the opposite direction and claim that (1) is false. In effect, the thought is that we have a kind of dialectical stand-off here between philosophy and commonsense, but that in the presence of such an impasse we are entitled to go with commonsense and thus reject the philosophical (i.e. sceptical) conclusion that we lack everyday knowledge.

The second concession that Moore makes to the radical sceptic is to grant that he can't give an explanation of why (1) is false. Moore's claim is just that commonsense dictates that it *must* be false. After all, all parties to this dispute agree that at least one of the three claims that make up the radical sceptical puzzle must be false. And notice that denying any one of these three claims—including, for that matter, denying (3)—generates mystery, given how plausible each of them is when taken independently. So Moore's contention is that while the falsity of (1) is mysterious, since the falsity of *any* of these three claims would be mysterious, this is not in itself a count against rejecting (1).

How plausible is this Moorean response to the sceptical puzzle? Remember that in Chapter 2 we made the distinction between radical scepticism as a paradox and radical scepticism as a position. Construed in the latter way, radical scepticism involves actively claiming that we lack everyday knowledge—that is, it involves denying (3). Construed in the former way, as merely a paradox, however, then the radical sceptic doesn't argue for any specific claim at all, but merely highlights that we are independently committed to three claims that are inconsistent. As we noted in Chapter 2, radical scepticism construed as a paradox has fewer dialectical burdens than radical scepticism as a position, not least because it doesn't have to explain how one might coherently embrace a radial sceptical conclusion.

This distinction between radical scepticism as a paradox and radical scepticism as a position is very important when it comes to evaluating the persuasiveness of Moore's anti-sceptical stance. Insofar as we focus on radical scepticism as a position, then Moore's response can look quite plausible. Both Moore and the sceptic are claiming something highly counterintuitive—that we can know the denials of radical sceptical hypotheses, and that we know very little of what we take ourselves to know, respectively. Moreover, there does seem to be a fairly even dialectical stand-off when it comes to choosing between these two positions. The sceptic grants (1) and (2), and hence denies (3), while the Moorean grants (3) and (2), and hence concludes that (1) should be rejected. If the options do come down to a clash between philosophy and commonsense in this way, then why not opt for commonsense and hence reject the sceptical position that involves denying (3)?

The problems for Moore's approach start to become apparent, however, once we shift our attention to radical scepticism construed as a paradox rather than as a position. This is because we are not now trading off the virtues and vices of one proposal in light of a competing radical sceptical proposal. Instead, we are faced with a fundamental tension apparently arising out of our own conception of knowledge and trying to work out how best to resolve this tension. With that way of thinking about radical scepticism in mind, what possible philosophical comfort can we possibly gain by being told that (1) must be false, such that we can know the denials of radical sceptical hypotheses, if we are not also told how this could ever be the case? Remember, after all, that we have already seen that intuitively we cannot know the denials of radical sceptical hypotheses, which is why we ended up endorsing (1) in the first place.

This means that if we are to turn Moore's appeal to commonsense into a plausible anti-sceptical proposal—one that has application even to the radical sceptical paradox at any rate—then we need to combine it with an account of how (1) could be false. In particular, how could it be possible for us to know the denials of radical sceptical hypotheses? The challenge here is to explain how such knowledge could be possible given that radical sceptical hypotheses are in their nature indistinguishable from our everyday experiences. That's a tall order. Indeed, even if we could offer such an account, it would on the face of it involve a highly revisionary account of knowledge. The worry would then be that such a revisionary account is even less plausible than the claims that generated the radical sceptical puzzle in the first place. The concern would be that we remain more convinced by the radical sceptic's contention that there is something deeply amiss with our ordinary ways of thinking about knowledge than with the revisionary anti-sceptical proposal on offer.

Scepticism and context

A different kind of response to the sceptical problem involves the idea that perhaps there is some sort of context-shift in play in the sceptical reasoning. It can certainly feel as if something of this kind is happening when one first engages with the problem. As we just noted in our discussion of scepticism and commonsense, we don't usually even consider radical sceptical hypotheses in our day-to-day life. Could it therefore be the case that the radical sceptic is somehow illicitly raising the standards for knowledge, and that this is what is generating the sceptical problem?

Here is one way of putting some flesh on the bones of this idea. Perhaps 'knows' is a context-sensitive term. The idea would be that sometimes this term is associated with a very undemanding epistemic standard, and hence is easy to satisfy, while at other times it is associated with a very demanding epistemic standard, and hence is hard (if not impossible) to satisfy. This could explain why our everyday usage of this term involves us ascribing lots of knowledge to each other, as the thought would be that in day-to-day contexts we use 'knows' in an undemanding way. Perhaps what happens when we engage with radical scepticism, however, is that we shift from using 'knows' in this undemanding way to employing it in its more austere rendering. It would thus be no surprise that we find ourselves no longer widely attributing knowledge, since 'knows' now means something far more restrictive than it did previously. Could the radical sceptical problem really turn on a shift of context of this kind?

It is certainly true that some of the words that we use are inherently context-sensitive, in the sense that one needs to know specific information about the situation in which they are used in order to work out what is meant. Perhaps the clearest example of this are indexicals, like 'I', 'here', and 'now'. When I say that 'I am hungry', I mean that *Duncan Pritchard* is hungry, but when you make the very same assertion you are making a claim about *you* and not about me. Understanding statements involving the word 'I' thus requires one to know who is speaking. Similarly, in order to understand what is meant by an assertion involving 'here' or 'now', it will be important to know when and where, respectively, the assertion was made. That expressions involving indexicals have this feature explains why no-one thinks that two people are disagreeing if one person says 'I am hungry' and the other person says 'I am not hungry'. If the same person made both assertions one after the other, then we would be puzzled, since they would seem to be contradicting themselves. But if two people make these assertions then there is no contradiction, since the 'I' in each case refers to a different person.

So there is clearly a precedent for there being terms in our language that are context-sensitive in roughly the way that it is being suggested that 'knows' might be. Indexicals are perhaps not the best examples to focus upon in this regard, however, as there is no appeal to standards in play here. In terms of 'I', for example, all that matters is who is speaking. But other context-sensitive terms do involve an appeal to standards. Take a term like 'tall', for example. I'm a couple of inches over 6 feet in height, and hence in most contexts I would count as tall. But in the context of picking a basketball team, however, I probably wouldn't count as tall at all. There is no contradiction here—it is not that I am simultaneously both tall and not tall. Rather, our assessments of tallness are made relative to a particular standard. At a couple of inches over 6 feet in height, I am tall relative to the standard of *average person* height, but that's not tall relative to the standard of *average basketball player* height. What goes here for 'tall' also applies to a range of other context-sensitive terms, like 'big', 'heavy', 'wide', 'empty', 'flat', and so on.

Could what is happening here with a term like 'tall' be what is occurring when we engage with radical scepticism? Just as it is ordinarily true to say that I am 'tall', since it is relative to an undemanding standard for tallness, so it is ordinarily true to say that we 'know' lots of things, since that is relative to an undemanding standard for knowledge. But just as it is not true to say that I am 'tall' relative to the demanding standards for tallness employed by (say) a basketball coach, so it is not true to say that I 'know' a lot of things relative to the more demanding standards for knowledge employed by the radical sceptic.

One advantage of this *contextualist* response to radical scepticism is that there is a sense in which both we're right *and* the sceptic is right. After all, our ordinary practices of ascribing knowledge to each other come out as correct, as they are implicitly picking out an undemanding standard for 'knows'. But the radical sceptic is also correct to contend, relative to the demanding standard for 'knows' that they employ, that we lack a lot of the knowledge that we take ourselves to have. This looked like we were contradicting each other, but insofar as 'knows' is a context-sensitive term then there is no more a contradiction in play here than that you are contradicting me when you say 'I am not hungry' just after I have declared 'I am hungry'.

Relatedly, the contextualist also has a way of claiming that, properly understood, the three claims that make up the radical sceptical paradox above are not really in conflict. Take (3), the claim that we have lots of everyday knowledge. According to contextualism, this is true relative to the everyday standards for 'knows', but false relative to the high standards for 'knows' employed by the radical sceptic. The contextualist can also explain why (1), the claim that we are unable to know the denials of radical sceptical hypotheses, is so compelling. After all, since (1) explicitly invokes radical sceptical hypotheses, it already brings in the problem of radical scepticism, and hence appeals to the demanding standards for 'knows' that the radical sceptic employs. If considering the problem of radical scepticism means raising the standards for 'knows', then evaluating whether we know the denials of radical sceptical hypotheses should be sufficient to take us into the more demanding sceptical context.

Conceding that (1) is true does not create any conflict with (3) and the closure principle, represented by (2), however, so long as we keep the relevant context fixed. In any high-standards context where (1) is at issue, then (3) is no longer true, and so there is no tension with the closure principle. That is, once we start thinking about radical sceptical hypotheses, as we would need to in order to evaluate (1), then we are in a sceptical context where 'knows' picks out a demanding standard. But in that context (3) is no longer true, as 'knows' there will also pick out a demanding standard as well. Put another way, we don't 'know' everyday claims relative to demanding sceptical standards.

And in any context where (3) comes out as true—where we do 'know' everyday claims, relative to the relevant undemanding standards—then the problem of radical scepticism is by definition not under consideration, and hence neither are radical sceptical hypotheses. Thus the question of whether (1) is true simply doesn't arise, and so there is no tension with the closure principle (and thus (2)). As soon as the question of whether (1) is true does arise, however, then (1) becomes true. But then (3) becomes false, as the standards for 'knows' have just risen to mean that we no longer 'know' everyday claims either.

Either way, then, there is no single context where the closure principle generates a tension between (1) and (3). Thus although it looked like claims (1)–(3) were jointly inconsistent, according to the contextualist this is not the case. What we have failed to do is realize that 'knows' is a context-sensitive term in the way that the contextualist has set out.

One might think that contextualism offers an elegant way of dealing with the problem of radical scepticism. But it faces some fairly serious objections. One kind of concern is that it is hard to understand why we were ever taken in by the problem of radical scepticism if contextualism is the right way to respond to it. No-one was ever confused about how what is meant by expressions involving indexicals could depend on context. Similarly, no-one has been led astray by the fact that words like 'tall' can be used in very different ways relative to different contexts of use. Put another way, there is no parallel sceptical puzzle involving 'I' or 'tall'. No-one gets puzzled, for example, that I count as tall relative to the standards for tallness employed in everyday contexts but that I don't count as tall relative to the standards employed by basketball coaches.

But if we are not confused by our usage of other context-sensitive terms, then why is 'knows' so different? That is, why didn't we recognize immediately that there was a context-shift going on in the radical sceptical argument, just as we do when it comes to our usage of other context-sensitive terms? Is it really plausible that a

Defending knowledge

puzzle that has perplexed philosophers for such a long time simply turns on a simple feature of language that we would ordinarily identify in a flash? Remember too in this regard that 'knows' is a pretty basic term, one that we are all familiar with—it's not as if it's an arcane word, or that it has a very specialized meaning.

There is another reason for thinking that contextualism doesn't get to the bottom of the radical sceptical problem. For the contextualist response to radical scepticism to gain a purchase on this difficulty, then it is crucial that we satisfy *some* epistemic standard for knowledge, albeit only a weak one. After all, the contextualist line is precisely that in everyday contexts our knowledge ascriptions are correct because the standards in play are so undemanding. This is how it can come out as true that I 'know' something so mundane as that I am currently wearing a shirt.

The problem, however, is that the radical sceptical problem that we posed earlier seems to exclude even this possibility. Remember that the radical sceptical puzzle was posed at the level of knowledge. In particular, the claim was that even if our beliefs are true, they do not amount to knowledge because we have no epistemic reason at all for thinking that our beliefs are true. As we noted, in normal circumstances I might think that I have all sorts of epistemic reasons for thinking, say, that I am wearing a shirt, but once the closure principle and radical sceptical hypotheses like the BIV scenario are in play, then these epistemic reasons seem to be shown to be illusory. After all, I know that if I were a BIV, then I wouldn't be wearing a shirt, but I don't know that I'm not a BIV. So how can I have any good epistemic reasons for thinking that I am wearing a shirt right now? Aren't my epistemic reasons for believing that I'm wearing a shirt right now the very same reasons that the BIV would offer for thinking that they are wearing a shirt? But if that's right, then in what sense do I have any good epistemic reasons at all?

The point is that insofar as radical scepticism generates this result, then contextualism is simply irrelevant to the problem in hand. This is because it would follow that we don't satisfy *any* standard for knowledge, not even the weakest standard imaginable. Accordingly, appealing to standards for 'knows' gains us no purchase on the sceptical problem whatsoever, as the difficulty is still with us. In short, we still lack knowledge, even relative to the low everyday standards described by the contextualist. And if we lack knowledge even relative to these undemanding epistemic standards, then we lack it *simpliciter*, just as the radical sceptic alleges.

Inverting scepticism

A more radical approach to the problem of radical scepticism is sketched by Ludwig Wittgenstein (1889–1951) in his final notebooks, published posthumously as *On Certainty* (1969). As we noted above, Wittgenstein's contemporary Moore thought that our everyday commonsense certainties had a special role to play in our response to radical scepticism. So did Wittgenstein, but his conception of the special role they are meant to play is radically different. Whereas Moore thought that these commonsense certainties provided us with a sound epistemic basis to push back against radical sceptical doubt, Wittgenstein instead claimed that they were essentially *arational* (i.e. neither rationally nor irrationally held). Let's try to unpack this thought, and why Wittgenstein thought that it provided us with anything constructive to say about radical scepticism. After all, on the face of it, to say that our most basic convictions are arationally held sounds an awful lot like Wittgenstein was *agreeing* with the radical sceptic.

In order to understand what Wittgenstein was proposing, we first need to step back a little and make a few observations about *rational evaluations*. We have previously noted that knowledge is true belief that is appropriately grounded in epistemic reasons. When we make rational evaluations—for example, when we try to determine whether a belief has the right kind of rational support such that it amounts to knowledge—we normally do so against a backdrop of accepted claims that are not themselves in question. So, for example, suppose we want to work out whether someone's belief that the tree that they are looking at is an oak amounts to knowledge. To do so we will consider various epistemically relevant factors. These might include why they believe what they do (e.g. is it because of the way the tree looks or is it based on someone else's testimony?); how responsible they are in forming their belief (e.g. did they inspect the tree closely, or merely take a quick glance at it?); how likely it would be that this person could be wrong about this subject matter (e.g. are there types of tree in the vicinity that look like oaks but which aren't oaks?); and so on. In undertaking a rational evaluation in this way we are evaluating whether one belief (in this case about whether this tree is an oak) amounts to knowledge relative to a background of claims that are already accepted as knowledge (e.g. that the tree looks like a typical oak tree; that there aren't non-oak trees in the vicinity that look like oaks; that one can spot an oak just by looking at it without the need for special checks; and so on). This is the sense in which rational evaluations are normally *local* in that we are not rationally evaluating all of our beliefs all at once, but only a sub-set of those beliefs, relative to a wider set of beliefs that are not in doubt (and which are thus treated as knowledge).

In contrast, the radical sceptic's rational evaluations are not local in this way, but *global*. After all, the radical sceptic is trying to determine whether our beliefs *as a whole* enjoy appropriate epistemic grounds, and so amount to knowledge. Indeed, that's just the whole point of introducing radical sceptical scenarios, which are precisely situations in which one's beliefs are massively in error (but which are nonetheless indistinguishable from normal life, which is why we are unable to rule them out).

Normally we rule out error-possibilities by appealing to things that we know that are not themselves called into question by that error-possibility. For example, one might rule out the error-possibility that the tree before one is not an oak but rather an elm by pointing out that one knows the difference between the appearances of these two trees, and hence can tell them apart. Here we are appealing to our knowledge (in this case of what oaks and elms look like) in order to rule out the error-possibility that what we think is an oak is actually an elm.

We cannot coherently take this kind of line with radical sceptical scenarios, however. This is because they are error-possibilities that call all (or at least most anyway) of one's beliefs into question, and hence call into question even one's background knowledge. That's why we cannot appeal to our memories or experiences (or even our beliefs about the current technological state-of-play) in order to rule out the BIV sceptical hypothesis, as this very scenario raises doubts about their veracity.

That radical scepticism is in the business of undertaking global rational evaluations rather than the local ones that we are ordinarily familiar with is not in itself a count against it. As we noted when we discussed the relevance of commonsense when it comes to the problem of radical scepticism, the radical sceptic is plausibly offering us a 'purified' version of our everyday practices. Normally we rationally evaluate our beliefs in a piecemeal fashion, and it makes sense to do so, given the practical constraints that we ordinarily operate under. We just don't have the time, much less the inclination, to question all our beliefs at once. But when we do philosophy we are not constrained by such limitations, and hence we can ask what the epistemic standing of our beliefs is as a whole. The radical sceptic's contention is that once we step back to do this we discover that our beliefs have no sound epistemic basis at all, and hence do not amount to knowledge (or, at least, that we don't have any plausible story available to us as to why they amount to knowledge).

Interestingly, it is not just the radical sceptic who attempts to rationally evaluate our beliefs as a whole. For notice that this is also the goal of the traditional *anti*-sceptic too. While the radical sceptic rationally evaluates our beliefs as a whole in a *negative* fashion, and so finds them wanting, the traditional anti-sceptic rationally evaluates our beliefs as a whole with a view to producing a *positive* verdict (i.e. as showing that they amount to knowledge, *contra* the radical sceptic). Recall that Descartes was trying to do this with his foundationalism, whereby we are able to show that our beliefs as a whole are in good epistemic order since they are supported by indubitable foundations. Moore was trying to do something in the same broad vein by appealing to our commonsense certainties. In particular, he was trying to show that such certainties provide us with a rational basis to push back against radical scepticism and thereby assure ourselves that our beliefs, as a whole, are perfectly in order from a rational point of view just as they are. (Or, at least, that if there is anything wrong with our beliefs in this regard, it is not something that the radical sceptic has exposed.)

This is where Wittgenstein's proposal comes in. His basic idea was that both the radical sceptic and the traditional anti-sceptic are employing a false conception of the nature of rational evaluation. In particular, Wittgenstein argued that it is not an *incidental* feature of our everyday rational evaluations that they are local. Instead, it is rather part of the very nature of rational evaluation that it is localized in this way. In particular, he claimed that the very idea that one could undertake a global rational evaluation—that is, to rationally evaluate all of one's beliefs all at once—is simply incoherent. If that's right, then both the radical sceptic and the traditional anti-sceptic are making the same fundamental error.

The reason why Wittgenstein made this claim was that he thought that all rational evaluations necessarily take place against a backdrop of a kind of primitive, but absolute, certainty. Since this certainty is needed for rational evaluations to occur, it is sometimes called a 'hinge' certainty, following a famous metaphor

8. **Hinges. Wittgenstein used the metaphor of a hinge to explain the special enabling role that he thought our most fundamental commitments play in our rational practices, while not being themselves subject to rational evaluation.**

that Wittgenstein employs in this regard (Figure 8). Consider this passage from *On Certainty*:

> [...] the *questions* that we raise and our *doubts* depend upon the fact that some propositions are exempt from doubt, are as it were like hinges on which those turn.
>
> That is to say, it belongs to the logic of our [...] investigations that certain things are *in deed* not doubted.
>
> But it isn't that the situation is like this: We just *can't* investigate everything, and for that reason we are forced to rest content with assumption. If I want the door to turn, the hinges must stay put.

Wittgenstein's point is that the very practice of rationally evaluating our beliefs presupposes these hinge certainties that enable rational evaluations to occur, and which are thus not themselves subject to rational evaluation. This hinge certainty is in effect an underlying tacit conviction that one is not radically in error. Wittgenstein held that this is manifested in the kind of brute certainty that we exhibit when it comes to those everyday claims that are, for us, optimally certain.

The contrast with Moore in this regard is instructive in that both of them are interested in the special role that our everyday certainties play, but with a crucial difference. While Moore thought that these everyday certainties had a special rational status (which enables us to push back against radical scepticism), Wittgenstein instead held that they are immune to rational evaluation. Not only can we make no sense of them being rationally grounded, but they are not thereby irrational either. They are rather the hinges that must be in place in order for rational evaluations to occur, and hence cannot themselves be rationally evaluated. If this is right, then it follows that there cannot be universal rational evaluations, since there will always need to be the hinge certainties in place for any rational evaluation to occur, and which are themselves immune to rational evaluation.

Let's consider an example that Wittgenstein discusses in this respect. As we noted above, Moore famously offered his belief that he has hands as one of the commonsense claims that he was optimally certain of. Thus, if any philosophical argument, like the radical sceptical puzzle that we have encountered, purports to show that he doesn't know he has hands, then Moore contends that it is more reasonable to reject that reasoning than to accept that he doesn't know that he has hands. In particular, as we saw above, it would seem that what Moore would have to claim is that we must be able to know the denials of radical sceptical hypotheses (even though he would grant that he cannot explain how). Wittgenstein agrees that this claim that one has hands is optimally certain for us, at least in normal conditions, but he doesn't think that this bestows it with any special rational status as Moore does. Wittgenstein argues that the fact that this is so certain for us in normal conditions means that we can neither make sense of there being any coherent grounds for doubting it or for there being any coherent grounds in favour of believing it.

We might think this is puzzling, since isn't my belief that I have hands something that is grounded in my experiences of my hands, my seeing them and feeling them and so forth? Wittgenstein contends that this is a mistake. As he puts it:

> If a blind man were to ask me 'Have you got two hands?' I should not make sure by looking. If I were to have any doubt of it, then I don't know why I should trust my eyes. For why shouldn't I test my *eyes* by looking to find out whether I see my two hands? *What* is to be tested by *what*?

The point is that such a certainty is not something that is itself rationally evaluated, but rather part of the unquestioned backdrop against which other claims are rationally evaluated. It is thus what makes rational evaluations possible in the first place. (Compare one's conviction that one has hands with one's conviction that one's keys are in one's pocket. If someone asks you if you have your keys, it makes perfect sense to tap one's sides to see if the tell-tale jingle of the keys in your pocket is there, or even to take them out to show the other person. But it makes no sense at all if someone asks you whether you have hands to produce them and say, 'Oh yes, here they are!').

Wittgenstein's point is that these everyday certainties manifest our general conviction that we are not fundamentally mistaken in our beliefs. But that we are not fundamentally mistaken in our beliefs is not something that we have any reason for holding. It is rather just part of what it is to be a believer, and for that matter a doubter, in the first place (Figure 9).

If we have no rational basis for these hinge certainties, then it follows that they can't be known, at least if we continue to

9. Faith and doubt. The interplay between faith and reason, and in particular with regard to how the former is meant to be reconciled with doubt, is a central motif of many religions, as depicted here by Caravaggio's masterpiece, 'The Incredulity of Saint Thomas' (*c*.1602).

maintain that knowledge requires true belief grounded in appropriate epistemic reasons. But one might wonder why this claim doesn't just collapse into radical scepticism. If our rational evaluations presuppose a hinge certainty that is lacking in rational support, then doesn't that mean that our beliefs are ultimately completely groundless (i.e. completely lacking in epistemic reasons)? Isn't that akin to conceding that what lies at the heart of our beliefs is just a matter of *faith*? The problem, however, is that faith seems to be *opposed* to reason. Accordingly, if at root our beliefs come down to faith, then it is hard to see why that doesn't simply entail that we don't know anything, just as the radical sceptic contends.

Notice, however, that while it's true on the Wittgensteinian picture that we don't have knowledge of the hinge certainties, there's also a sense in which we don't fail to know them either. That is, this is not something that we are ignorant of, as if it is something that we could have known but failed to. Wittgenstein's claim is that there is no sense to the idea of a rational evaluation that didn't presuppose this backdrop of hinge certainty, and hence that one cannot rationally evaluate the hinge itself as this needs to be in place for a rational evaluation to occur. The hinge certainty is thus in a sense neither something that we could know nor something that we could fail to know (i.e. be ignorant of)—it simply isn't the kind of thing that is in the market for knowledge.

This marks a subtle difference between Wittgenstein's proposal and radical scepticism. They both agree that the hinge certainty is unknown, but the explanation is different in each case. For Wittgenstein, it is unknown because the hinge certainty is simply not the kind of thing that could be known, and it is a philosophical mistake to think otherwise. For the radical sceptic, in contrast, the hinge certainty is the kind of claim that could be known, it is just that we have failed to know it (i.e. we are ignorant of it). Although subtle, this difference is important. If we are simply ignorant of the hinge certainty, then the idea that our everyday beliefs, buttressed by local rational evaluations, lack supporting epistemic reasons looks very plausible. But if the hinge certainty is not even in the market for knowledge, then why should the fact that it is unknown have any negative ramifications for the epistemic pedigree of our everyday beliefs? This is why I have described this Wittgensteinian approach as 'inverting' scepticism in that it takes a key contention that the radical sceptic makes and attempts to turn it on its head so that it can be employed against radical scepticism.

Even if one grants this point to Wittgenstein, however, it can still look mysterious how this anti-sceptical line is to have any application to the particular formulation of the radical sceptical puzzle that we are dealing with. On the face of it, the idea seems to be that our basic certainty that we are not radically in error is encapsulated in our conviction that we are not the victims of radical sceptical hypotheses. Sure, one might go through the motions of entertaining such scenarios, of thinking that one might be a BIV for example, but the certainty that is manifest in our day-to-day actions reveals that there is in fact no doubt in play here at all. So, just as the radical sceptic contends, we don't know the denials of radical sceptical hypotheses, in line with (1), though with the proviso that we are not ignorant of such claims either. And yet, the thinking seems to go, the epistemic support enjoyed by our everyday beliefs is perfectly in order as it is, even though this is the product of local rational evaluations that take place against a backdrop of primitive arational certainty. The Wittgensteinian position thus seems to endorse (3) as well.

So does that mean that the Wittgensteinian line involves denying (2), and hence rejecting the closure principle? It can certainly seem that this must be implied by this approach, since what other option is there? The thought appears to be that the closure principle looks innocuous because we are implicitly taking it as given that there can be universal rational evaluations. Ordinarily, the closure principle will only take you from one locally evaluated piece of knowledge to another locally evaluated piece of knowledge, as when one concludes from the fact that the tree is an oak that it is not an elm (given that one knows that no tree is both an oak and an elm). What is distinctive about instances of the closure principle that the radical sceptic employs, however, is that they take us from everyday, locally evaluated, knowledge claims to the denials of radical sceptical hypotheses, where the latter are the kind of thing which, if known, would involve a global rational evaluation. The Wittgensteinian line on closure thus seems to be the thought that instances of the closure principle of this kind are far from innocuous in that they presuppose a conception of the nature of rational evaluation which Wittgenstein maintains is completely false.

If that's right, then the Wittgensteinian response to the problem of rational scepticism is to deny the closure principle, and thus (2).

But given the evident plausibility of the closure principle, this is going to be a difficult approach to take, as it inevitably involves denying something that we find highly intuitive.

The state of play

My goal in this chapter has not been to argue for any particular response to the problem of radical scepticism, or even to offer a comprehensive overview of all the responses available. Instead, I've presented a representative sample of anti-sceptical proposals so that the reader can get a sense of how one might go about approaching this difficulty. As we have seen, all of the anti-sceptical lines we have looked have their own difficulties, with no account offering us a 'slam-dunk' on this score. Does that mean that the situation is hopeless? Not at all. In fact, that there are a range of responses available, each with their own merits and demerits, is entirely normal for a philosophical puzzle, and hence is nothing to be surprised about. What it tells us is that the puzzle in hand is likely to be deep and important, such that rather than being amenable to a straightforward solution it instead prompts us to look more closely at the subject matter in question, and in the process refine our thinking about it. In the case of the radical sceptical paradox, this could mean, for example, trying to make sense of how our system of rational evaluation might necessarily incorporate arational hinge commitments (as Wittgenstein suggested), or figuring out how 'knowledge' could be a context-sensitive notion in disguise (as the contextualism contends). The point of considering these anti-sceptical lines is thus not to convince you of a particular solution, much less to convince you that there is no solution available, but rather to demonstrate that there are philosophically interesting responses that can be offered to the problem of radical scepticism. With this in mind, it would be just as premature to throw in the towel to radical scepticism as it would be to opt for one of these anti-sceptical proposals and declare victory.

Chapter 4
Scepticism as a way of life

We began this book by noting a distinction between a healthy, moderate scepticism and a radical scepticism that had all kinds of challenging implications. The former is the antidote to gullibility in that it prompts us to question what we are told and not merely to take it at face value. Such moderate scepticism is thus to be encouraged. Where scepticism becomes problematic is when it slips into the more radical variety. Whereas a moderate scepticism scrutinizes particular claims, a radical scepticism is sceptical about the truth of our beliefs *en masse*. This has troubling ramifications, as we saw in Chapter 1. If all our beliefs are open to question, then why be committed to the truth of anything? Moreover, once we determine that we have no grip on the truth, then why should it matter any more what is true? Radical scepticism thus invites relativism about truth, such that the truth is no longer something objective, but just whatever someone claims the truth to be.

But what are the motivations for radical scepticism? Those who express a radical scepticism—or its close cousin, relativism—in public life rarely offer any theoretical basis for it. Think, for example, of those who question the authority of science, who offer wholesale conspiracy theories, who happily assert that contemporary politics is in a 'post-truth' phase, and so on. These claims, which presuppose radical scepticism/relativism, do not bring with them any justification for this presupposition.

We saw in Chapter 1 that some of the rationales that might be offered for radical scepticism are in fact highly dubious. For example, the undeniable fact that we are fallible creatures who are sometimes in error does not in itself offer a justification for radical scepticism. That we are sometimes mistaken does not mean that we are always mistaken. Similarly, that we hardly ever, if ever, have reasons to be completely certain in what we believe is not a rationale for radical doubt either. The point is that human knowledge doesn't demand infallibility or complete certainty, and hence that our beliefs lack these features doesn't show that they fail to amount to knowledge.

That knowledge doesn't entail infallibility or complete certainty was also why radical scepticism doesn't follow directly from the fact that we cannot rule out radical sceptical hypotheses. Recall that these are scenarios, like the BIV scenario, where one is radically deceived about the world around one, but undetectably so. It seems that by definition we cannot come to know that we are not in such a scenario. But this by itself doesn't have any radical sceptical implications. It just reminds us that there is always the possibility of error, and that's just to reiterate the point that we are fallible—and hence to some degree quite rightly uncertain—creatures.

Interestingly, however, although appeals to infallibility and complete certainty are not motivations for radical scepticism, they do offer rationales for moderate scepticism. If we are sometimes mistaken, and are often not in a position to be completely confident of what we believe, then of course we should be careful about what beliefs we endorse.

Indeed, this is precisely why we find a moderate scepticism at work in the scientific method, because scientists recognize that our means of finding the truth are imperfect. This is why even well-founded scientific claims are nonetheless treated as provisional, in the sense of being open to being reevaluated if new evidence comes to light. Far from science representing a dogmatic stance about the world around us, the scientific method in fact *incorporates* such a moderate scepticism.

Indeed, the emergence of what we now think of as the scientific method during the period of history known as the scientific revolution (roughly from the middle of the 16th century to the 18th century) is widely regarded as being in large part due to the rediscovery of ancient sceptical texts during the Renaissance. By questioning the received wisdom of the past, and in particular the authority of the Church which was often appealed to as underpinning this received wisdom, scientists were able to discover new and important truths, such as that the sun did not orbit the earth as previously supposed, and much else besides (Figure 10). Interestingly, however, while radical forms of scepticism did emerge in this period, the ancient forms of scepticism that our new scientists were responding to at this time are more concerned with localized forms of doubt. In examining this period of history we are thus witnessing how a moderate scepticism can be harnessed to *enhance* our grip on the truth, and in the process spur the kind of scientific progress that we now take for granted.

That said, we also noted in Chapter 2 that there is a powerful argument that can be offered in support of radical scepticism. This employs radical sceptical hypotheses, but doesn't rest only on appealing to these scenarios (since it also makes use of the closure principle). We also saw in Chapter 3 that while there are philosophical responses to this argument, they all face problems of their own.

Significantly, however, this radical sceptical argument is never presented by those in public life who exhibit such radical sceptical

10. Faith versus science. The trial of Galileo by the Roman Catholic Inquisition in the first half of the 17th century (here depicted by Cristiano Banti, 1857), for the putative heresy of defending heliocentrism, highlighted the clash between the authority of the Church and the new science.

tendencies, and this is no accident. Part of the reason for this, of course, is that those who espouse radical scepticism in public life are probably unfamiliar with the philosophical ideas behind it. But even if they were aware of the radical sceptical paradox, they would still be unwise to try to use it to motivate their particular sceptical stance. This is because far from supporting their scepticism, it would instead serve to undermine it by exposing just how radical the scope of their doubt is.

Consider someone who advances a general scepticism about science, who thinks that human-caused climate change is a hoax, that vaccines are part of a global conspiracy to harm our children, and so on. As we've previously noted, once one's scepticism becomes this broad, then it is hard to see how it could be contained—if one is sceptical about science, then why not be sceptical about everything? Accordingly, one might think that an argument that purports to show that knowledge is impossible would be a boon to such a person. The problem, however, is that it is in fact important to our science sceptic that they *don't* generalize their doubt in this way. After all, they want to maintain that they are in a privileged epistemic position relative to everyone else; that they can see through the conspiracy that everyone else is falling for. But that means that they need to credit themselves with knowledge that others are lacking, and hence a truly radical scepticism is not their friend. Our science sceptic is thus trying to pull off a kind of intellectual high-wire act, whereby they advance a dramatic form of scepticism which is nonetheless not quite so dramatic that it thereby also undermines the knowledge that they need to advance their case in the first place.

Such an intellectual high-wire act is not sustainable, as we've previously noted. Once one's doubt becomes extensive enough, then it also undermines one's own grounds for doubt and hence becomes self-destructive. This doesn't mean that there is no problem of radical scepticism, only that this problem is not best understood as a position—that is, as a view that someone coherently advances—as opposed to being a puzzle or paradox. In any case, this is why there would be nothing to be gained by our science sceptic (or anyone else in public life who advances a sufficiently general form of scepticism) by appealing to the radical sceptical paradox in support of their stance. To do so would expose just how radical the scepticism in play is, and thereby undermine it.

This point highlights how radical scepticism when advanced in public life (as opposed to in a philosophical discussion) is in a certain sense *fake*. Our science sceptic is happy to advance doubts that call most of what we believe into question, while nonetheless trying to maintain that their grounds for such doubts are entirely secure and beyond doubt. But that's simply not credible. Moreover, this kind of intellectual 'double-dealing' is also manifest in how our science sceptic lives their life. Such a person is usually quite content to receive first-world healthcare, to travel on planes with the confidence that they won't fall out of the sky, and so on. But if they are really a sceptic about science, then how can that be the case?

The crucial point is that once we make explicit what radical scepticism involves, then it is hard, if not impossible, to even make sense of someone adopting this as a stance. How should we make sense of someone who claims not to believe anything? How do we make sense of what they do, what they care about—including the radically sceptical claims that they make—and so forth if we take them seriously as being genuinely sceptical about everything? This is why those who espouse radical sceptical ideas in public life do not express them in these terms (even though they implicitly trade on sceptical themes), since to do so would be contrary to their purposes in advancing their scepticism in the first place. They want us to believe *them*, after all, even if they don't want us to believe much else.

Interestingly, similar points apply when it comes to those who put forward relativistic ideas about truth in public life, as this also involves a healthy dose of fakery. Those who try to convince us that objective truth doesn't matter in political life, for example, because there is no such thing as objective truth, are not in fact giving up on an objective conception of truth at all. Do you think that their lack of concern for the objective truth extends to matters of practical concern to them? For example, do you think they would be so sanguine about what is objectively true if it were the tax authorities declaring that they were not due the tax refund to which they are entitled? Or if they were falsely accused of a serious crime? This is the sense in which their commitment to relativism is fake, since if they really were relativists about truth then they wouldn't regard anything as objectively true. Like those who advance radical sceptical ideas in public life, these relativists are trying to pull off an intellectual high-wire act, whereby they are relativists about objective truth when it suits them but not when it doesn't. Such a position is no more sustainable in this case than it was with our science sceptic.

These points about the incoherence of radical sceptical and relativistic ideas in public life highlight something important. For often these ideas are presented as being challenges to authority, and thus as liberating narratives that one can employ to undermine existing power-structures. In fact, the reality is almost always the opposite in that such ideas in fact serve to support existing power structures and keep them in place—authority has nothing to fear from them. For example, if science is totally debunked, then why should we listen to scientists who demand action on human-caused climate change? Or if there is no such thing as objective truth, then it also cannot be an objective matter that there is injustice in society. But how then could one consistently advance any political basis for confronting such injustice?

In any case, the argument for radical scepticism that we looked at in Chapter 2 was powerful precisely because it was not essentially tied to a radical sceptical *position*. Rather, it was primarily put forward as a *paradox*—that is, as exposing deep tensions within our own concept of knowledge. As we saw, paradoxes can be coherently posed without this requiring anyone to advocate for a particular way of resolving that paradox. Radical scepticism as a paradox is thus distinct from radical scepticism as a position—that is, as a lived stance that one takes. That the latter often leads to incoherence thus doesn't entail that there is anything essentially amiss with the former.

Those who espouse radical sceptical and relativistic ideas in public life are therefore unable to legitimately appeal to the radical sceptical paradox in support of their claims. Moreover, as we also saw in Chapter 3, just as a case can be made in support of this paradox, there are also philosophical responses that can be offered. It would therefore be premature to conclude that there is an insolvable sceptical problem afflicting our knowledge.

In what follows we are going to be putting radical scepticism to one side and considering instead how one might make a positive case for a moderate scepticism. To this end we will be looking at an idea that we get from the ancients, and in particular from the work of possibly the greatest philosopher who ever lived, Aristotle (384–322 BCE; Figure 11). This idea concerns the role of the *virtues*, and the *intellectual virtues* in particular, in the 'good life' of *human flourishing*; what the ancient Greeks called *eudaimonia*. As we will see, understanding the role that the intellectual virtues play in the good life will enable us to see how

11. **Aristotle. The ancient Greek thinker Aristotle presented a systematic philosophical picture, with the virtues at its heart, that is still influential today.**

embracing a moderate scepticism could be necessary for living such a life (in contrast to embracing radical scepticism, which would be inimical to it). Relatedly, it will also help us to resolve a possible tension between adopting a healthy moderately sceptical attitude while at the same time living a life of genuine conviction.

Intellectual virtues and vices

Philosophers are often accused of being focused on entirely abstract matters, unconnected with the pressing issues that confront us in everyday life. This certainly wasn't true of Aristotle, however, who was concerned to offer us practical advice about how to lead good lives. When we think of ethics in modern life we tend to equate it with morality—that is, with what is specifically morally good (and bad). But for Aristotle, as for many ancient philosophers, ethics had a much broader meaning as being concerned with the more general question of how one ought to live; what constitutes a good life. Morality may be part of such a life, but it is but one part, as there are other important elements to a good life. A life that is lacking in achievements, in significant personal relationships, or in aesthetic experience would be impoverished as a result, but none of these things are essentially concerned with morality. There thus might be more to living a good life than simply living a moral life. It is the broader ethical question of how to live a good life that Aristotle attempted to answer.

He approached this question by appealing to the role of the *virtues* in the good life. These are distinctive kinds of character traits—that is, dispositions that one has to behave in certain ways—that are particularly admirable. They include such traits as courage, generosity, and kindness. The virtues have a number of interesting properties, at least according to Aristotle. For example, virtues lie in opposition to *vices*, which are character traits that are not admirable at all (indeed, they are often contemptible). Indeed, a virtue lies between two vices, a vice of excess and a vice of deficiency. Take courage, for instance. The lack of courage—cowardice—is a vice, but one can also take excessive risks and thereby exhibit the very different vice of being rash or foolhardy. Being courageous is thus having the good judgement to be disposed to act between these two extremes, what Aristotle called the *golden mean*.

We are not born with virtues but must acquire them through practice, especially by emulating those around us who have these admirable traits. One has to learn to be courageous, as opposed to being cowardly or rash. And one needs to cultivate this virtue once acquired, or it is apt to be lost. It is properties like this that set virtues apart from mere skills. We can be born with certain skills (e.g. our hardwired skills to perceive our environment via our senses), and there can be skills that are learnt in such a way that they are unlikely to be lost regardless of whether one cultivates them thereafter (e.g. riding a bicycle). Another important difference between skills and virtues is that the latter bring with them distinctive kinds of motivations. Someone who has the virtue of generosity, for example, will be genuinely motivated to help others. Merely acting as if one has this virtue—in order to impress one's peers, for example—is not the same as being virtuous. Skills, in contrast, often don't demand motivations in this way. Indeed, being able to act in ways that give others the (false) impression that one is generous might well be a very skilful thing to do.

But the big difference between mere skills and virtues is that the latter have a special kind of value, and this is because of the vital role that they play in a good life. In essence, Aristotle held that the good life is the life of virtue. Notice that he isn't suggesting that such a life will be good in the sense that it will always involve pleasure rather than pain, or that it will be a life without conflict and suffering. In fact, Aristotle took it for granted that all lives were likely to involve pain, conflict, and suffering. The point is rather that the way to confront such ills is by being armed with the virtues. If one is kind, generous, courageous, and so on, then one can flourish as a human being despite facing such difficulties.

Moreover, facing these difficulties in such a virtuous manner is in any case far better than being insulated from them in an empty life of meaningless pleasure. Pleasure without virtue never turns out well, as I think we all know.

I noted that ethics for Aristotle is not just about morality, and this is reflected in the virtues themselves. Some of them, like kindness and generosity, do seem to be particularly moral. But others are less so, such as courage. In fact, Aristotle held that being virtuous didn't simply involve knowing what the right thing to do is from a moral point of view, but also consists in having the specifically *intellectual* virtues too. After all, how can one *know* the right thing to do if one doesn't have knowledge in the first place? And yet the intellectual virtues are vital to ensuring that one is a knower.

The intellectual virtues include such traits as *conscientiousness* and *open-mindedness*. They also include intellectual variants of more general kinds of virtue, as when someone is specifically *intellectually courageous* (think, for instance, of a scientist who develops a radical new idea) or when someone exhibits *intellectual humility* (as opposed to intellectual arrogance). So, for example, to be intellectually conscientious is to form one's beliefs by attending to all the relevant evidence and being able to appropriately weigh up this evidence in reaching a decision. It is just such a trait that we would want in a judge who was hearing our trial, for example, or in a doctor who was making a decision about whether we needed an operation. This intellectual virtue lies between two corresponding intellectual vices. On the one hand, there is the vice of deficiency of not attending to the evidence at all in reaching one's decision, but rather, for example, opting for whatever outcome suits your interests. On the other hand, there is also the vice of excess of being so attentive to all the evidence, regardless of its relevance to the issue in hand, that one is simply swamped and so unable to reach a decision. The golden mean involves having the wisdom to navigate between these two extremes.

Having this picture in play of how there is an intellectual element to the good life helps us to clarify how a radical scepticism would be inimical to such a life. It also helps us to see just what might be admirable about a localized scepticism. Let's take these points in turn. We have noted previously that there is a deep incoherency about trying to actively embrace radical scepticism. How can we even make sense of someone who claims not to know anything and to doubt everything? We have also noted that radical scepticism poses an existential challenge because our inability to know anything would make our lives absurd. The Aristotelian picture gives us the means to develop this last point. The idea that without knowledge our lives would be absurd is a purely negative claim in that it merely tells us that some essential component to a meaningful life would be lacking. In particular, it doesn't tell us how having knowledge might make our lives meaningful (perhaps they would still be absurd, but for different reasons). This is where the Aristotelian account of the virtues is helpful in that it offers a positive story about what is involved in a meaningful life, one that makes essential use of the intellectual virtues, and thus the knowledge that these virtues generate. In particular, given that manifesting the virtues requires knowledge, how could one lead a virtuous life if one doubts everything? For example, how could someone have the good judgement to be courageous and generous, and thereby know how best to act in this regard, while living such a life of radical doubt? The Aristotelian picture thus tells us why, if radical scepticism were true, then one's life would be lacking in a fundamental respect in that the life of flourishing, *eudaimonia*, would simply be unavailable.

Interestingly, however, while a life of radical scepticism is in conflict with the virtues, an attitude of moderate scepticism seems to be licensed by the virtues, particularly the intellectual virtues. Indeed, the intellectual virtues tend to characteristically involve a moderate scepticism. Isn't that part of what is involved in being *conscientious* when one weighs up the evidence, rather than leaping to conclusions? Or in being *open-minded* in one's opinions, as opposed to being dogmatic? Moderate scepticism is thus often what is dictated by the golden mean, where radical scepticism represents a vice of excess (i.e. of excessive doubt), with dogmatism representing the opposing vice of deficiency (i.e. of insufficient doubt). Accordingly, on an Aristotelian conception of the virtues, and of the intellectual virtues in particular, we can account for the importance of moderate scepticism by showing how it is conducive to a life of flourishing. Relatedly, we can also explain just what is problematic about attempting to live a life of radical scepticism, as this would be inimical to living such a flourishing life. (To reiterate our point from earlier, remember that in saying this we are not thereby claiming that the problem of radical scepticism *qua* paradox is thereby resolved. Radical scepticism as a position and radical scepticism as a paradox are very different beasts.)

Pyrrhonian scepticism

How far can one take the sceptical attitude without it being contrary to a life of flourishing? As we have just seen, on the Aristotelian ethical account there are limits, since the sceptical attitude needs to be in moderation if it is to be in tune with one's exercising of the virtues, especially the intellectual virtues, and yet being virtuous is vital to living the good life. Radical scepticism thus leads to vice (or at least away from virtue), rather than to virtue. But there is a different kind of ethical stance, also due to the ancients, that seems to embody sceptical ideas and in the process incorporate a more extensive form of sceptical doubt (though, as we will see, 'doubt' might not be the right word to use here). This is *Pyrrhonian scepticism*, and like the Aristotelian account we have just looked at it was also an ethical proposal about what constitutes the life of flourishing. Rather than appealing to the virtues, however, the Pyrrhonians thought that it was adopting a sceptical attitude that was key to living a good life.

How best to understand the Pyrrhonian stance is difficult, not least because it is in the nature of a lived scepticism of this kind that its adherents didn't write down their thoughts. (For why would a committed sceptic do that?) The movement itself is named after the ancient Greek philosopher Pyrrho of Elis (*c.*360–270 BCE), but what we know of his ideas is entirely second-hand, with much of it derived from the work of Sextus Empiricus (*c.*160–210 CE) and his *Outlines of Pyrrhonism*. Interestingly, one thing we do know about Pyrrho is that he took part in Alexander the Great's expedition to India, where he would likely have been exposed to the rich vein of philosophical ideas that were bubbling in that region at the time. This is significant, since it might explain why Pyrrhonian scepticism seems to have a particular affinity with Eastern philosophical traditions. In particular, as several commentators have pointed out, there are some intriguing parallels between Pyrrhonian sceptical thought and Madhyamaka Buddhism, as founded by the Indian philosopher, Nāgārjuna (*c.*150–250 CE).

One thing that we do know about the Pyrrhonians is that they weren't attempting to be radical sceptics who doubted everything. They recognized that in order to live one must have some commitments, and that tempered the extent of their scepticism. In particular, it was not our everyday spontaneous judgements that were the target of their scepticism, but rather theoretical claims that are at least partially divorced from everyday life.

With this in mind, the Pyrrhonians didn't advance any philosophical claims of their own, and hence don't put forward any sceptical arguments as such. As we have seen, advancing sceptical arguments involves making some quite specific theoretical claims, such as concerning the closure principle. Instead, what the Pyrrhonians offer are what are known as sceptical *modes*, which are essentially techniques designed to induce doubt (or suspension of judgement anyway—the importance of this caveat will become apparent in a moment). The idea is that, in response to someone putting forward a theoretical claim, one can employ these modes to oppose them, with the result that this would engender a neutral attitude (what the Greeks called *epoche*). This would, in turn—at least if the process were repeated enough times anyway—eventually lead to a tranquil and untroubled state of mind (what the Greeks called *ataraxia*). It is intellectual quietude of this kind that the Pyrrhonians thought constituted the good life, as opposed to the virtuous life described by Aristotle. The idea is that one needs to master the sceptical modes, which are like skills aimed at provoking doubt, and in the process attain the tranquillity of *ataraxia*.

Three of these sceptical modes have become particularly influential, to the extent that they have become known separately from the other modes as 'Agrippa's Trilemma' (after the 1st century Pyrrhonian sceptic Agrippa, who is credited with formulating them). In essence, the thought is that when someone puts forward a theoretical claim one can counter it by querying what reasons the person has in favour of this claim. It seems that there are only three ways that this exchange can pan out, and none of them would make the proposition in question very convincing. Suppose first that our interlocutor offers reasons in support of their claim. The problem is that these reasons are themselves further theoretical claims, and so one can reapply the sceptical modes to ask in turn what grounds them. Our interlocutor might respond by offering further reasons for doubt, but then of course we can challenge the new reasons, and so on. They are thus caught in an *infinite regress* in that there is in principle no end to how many times this challenge can be repeated as new grounds are offered. But how can an infinite regress of reasons support a claim? Alternatively, they might respond not by offering new grounds at all, but rather by repeating a reason that they had offered previously. The problem now is that this seems to show that their reasoning was in fact circular. But how could circular reasoning support a claim? Finally, they might well respond at some point by simply insisting that they cannot offer any further reasons for what they claim. But then it seems that their claim ultimately rests on unsupported foundations. But how could that be an adequate rational basis for belief? Agrippa's Trilemma is thus a way of apparently showing that any theoretical claim that one puts forward can ultimately be shown to either be groundless or else 'grounded' in reasoning that is either circular or involves an infinite regress. The result is that the claim in question is shown to enjoy no rational basis at all. The sceptical modes thus lead one to lose any conviction one might have had in the target proposition.

Notice that the Pyrrhonians do not conclude on this basis that no theoretical belief amounts to knowledge, since that would be itself to make a theoretical claim. This is why Pyrrhonism was often *contrasted* with the prevailing form of scepticism of the time, which was Academic scepticism. Indeed, Sextus Empiricus describes Pyrrhonism as offering an intermediate stance between dogmatism and (Academic) scepticism. The thought goes that while the dogmatists insist that we have knowledge, and the Academic sceptic claims that we lack knowledge, the Pyrrhonians instead just maintain that we should continue inquiring. This suggests that for the Pyrrhonians it is the idea of an open inquiry that is key. Just as we should avoid settled beliefs where we can, and always be open to the possibility of error, so we should avoid settled doubts where we can too, as both have a tendency to close down inquiry. On this reading Pyrrhonism is not primarily about generating doubt at all, but rather aimed at promoting the suspension of belief. (Interestingly, this way of thinking about Pyrrhonism is closer in spirit to what the original Greeks meant by the word 'sceptic', which refers more to an inquirer than a doubter—the idea that 'scepticism' is essentially about doubt is something that comes later. Moreover, the Greek term *epoche*, which characterizes the neutral attitude that is generated by the sceptical modes, is usually translated as suspension of judgement.)

On this way of thinking about Pyrrhonism, it is the activity of engaging in a genuinely open inquiry that is central to the good life of human flourishing. That's a very different conception of the good life to that advocated by Aristotle. One key way in which it is different is that its focus is specifically on intellectual concerns as the route to the good life, through the emphasis on the right kind of perpetually open inquiry. For Aristotle, in contrast, while contemplation and other intellectual goods are important to the good life of human flourishing, they are but one part of the recipe in this regard, as there is a great deal of other ingredients that are also important, including moral, practical, and aesthetic concerns. This is why Pyrrhonism can coherently incorporate a more extensive scepticism than the Aristotelian account, since on this view the ethical goal only concerns intellectual matters. The Pyrrhonians thus do not need to worry about their sceptical activities undermining other aspects of their lives, since they aren't important to living the good life as they conceive of it. In contrast, for the Aristotelian it is important to keep one's scepticism in check because it militates against one's manifestation of virtue more generally, such as one's capacity for kindness or courage. The general point in play here is that the richer and more multi-dimensional one's account of the good life is, the more restrictions it places on the scope of scepticism that could be compatible with it. Still, the moral remains that there are limits to the extent to which one can be sceptical and yet live the good life.

Scepticism, conviction, and the good life

Earlier I described how the intellectual virtues could be an essential part of a life of flourishing, a good life. I've also described how a moderate scepticism could be viewed as a manifestation of the intellectual virtues, unlike a radical scepticism. There is still an important puzzle remaining about how any kind of scepticism could be compatible with a life of flourishing. The crux of the matter is that we also treat *conviction* as being essential to a good life too. We want people to have, as we might put it, the strength of their convictions, to stick by their principles and not simply abandon their most cherished beliefs at the first sign of dissent. Arguably at least, someone who lacked conviction would be lacking something crucial to the good life of human flourishing. Indeed, isn't such conviction part of what it is to manifest the virtue of being intellectually courageous? But how can we square the importance of conviction to the good life with the apparently opposing role that we have described for moderate scepticism?

In order to see why this conflict is in fact illusory, we first need to unpack what is involved in conviction in this regard, at least insofar as it is a plausible part of a life of flourishing. To begin with, notice that there is nothing particularly laudable about people who stick to their convictions regardless of the rational support they have for those beliefs, or whether they even have any rational support for them (Figure 12). Merely holding onto one's beliefs no matter what looks like mere dogmatism, and it is hard to see why that would be an important part of a life of flourishing (much less that it has anything to do with the manifestation of intellectual virtue).

Relatedly, in saying that we want people to be willing to stick to their convictions in the face of dissent, I take it that what we mean is that we want people to not simply give up their convictions because of pressure from other people. For example, if someone who holds anti-racist views finds themselves surrounded by people expressing racist opinions, we would think it disappointing if they 'went with the flow' and duly parroted the racist views of those around them. One reason why this would be disappointing is that it would display a willingness to change one's mind *even though one has been given no reason for doing so*, but merely because it is convenient (in this case socially convenient). In contrast, sometimes one is given excellent reasons to change one's mind, and when this happens one ought to do so. Being willing to change one's mind when one has been given good reasons for doing so is not a sign that one lacks conviction, but rather

12. Conviction and public reason. While we might want our political leaders to have conviction, such conviction can be dangerous when cut free from reason and put to use by a demagogue.

demonstrates that one is rational. This is certainly something that the intellectually virtuous person would do.

Just as we would find it disappointing if someone abandoned their beliefs merely due to social pressure, so we would find it disheartening if someone were to change their mind when offered only very weak reasons for doing so. If one has formed one's beliefs appropriately, and hence has good reasons in support of them, then one ought not to change one's mind at the first sign of any argument against one's views, no matter how flimsy. Indeed, if one has really thought through why one is so convinced about this subject matter, then one should be able to rebut weak counterevidence were it to be offered—for example, if someone offers a manifestly implausible justification for their opposing views. It follows that there is no inherent reason why someone who has conviction in their beliefs should be unwilling to listen to counterevidence to their views.

So insofar as conviction is laudable, and thus the kind of thing that might be part of the good life of human flourishing, then it ought to be grounded in reasons and it should be open to counterevidence. Call this *reasonable conviction*. We can thus set aside types of unreasonable conviction that are merely dogmatic, where this means either not grounded in reasons or closed off from counterevidence (or both). Reasonable conviction seems part of an intellectually virtuous life. Indeed, it seems to be something that is entirely compatible with one embracing the kind of moderate scepticism that we noted above. That requires that one is suitably sensitive to reasons, but as we just described it that's precisely what a reasonable conviction involves.

Even with the scope of conviction so restricted, there is still a puzzle here. If one has really thought through the issues and arrived at a certain conclusion, then doesn't that mean that the matter is settled? If so, then why should one consider counterevidence? (And if it isn't settled, then doesn't that mean that conviction isn't warranted?) Indeed, if one takes oneself to have impeccable rational support for a particular claim, then isn't that in itself a good reason to regard any evidence against that claim as being misleading? Conversely, if one does take such counterevidence seriously, then doesn't that mean downgrading one's own conviction accordingly? After all, if responding to such counterevidence seriously doesn't entail downgrading one's conviction, then doesn't that mean that one simply isn't taking it seriously, but is rather (perhaps secretly) adopting a dogmatic stance?

We can bring this point out by considering cases of disagreement. Imagine that you have a certain political view, a position which you have thought through rationally over a long time. Suppose you are now confronted by a group of people who, it turns out, have also thought through these matters but have come to the exact opposite conclusion. Since they have also thoroughly contemplated these issues, they are able to marshal counterarguments of their own, counterarguments that aren't obviously flawed. How should you respond? In particular, what does having reasonable conviction in your views demand of you?

One might think that having reasonable conviction here means being unwilling to even consider these counterarguments. After all, you have thought through these issues and come to a conclusion. The matter is thus settled for you. But as we noted above, that sort of response does seem dogmatic.

After all, can't reasonable people come to very different opinions, especially regarding such a contentious subject matter as politics? If that's so, isn't that a reason to show a little *humility* and not be so sure of one's own opinions? But that seems to suggest that the alternative to sticking to one's guns in the face of disagreement is to downgrade one's confidence in one's beliefs. But how does that allow any intellectual space for reasonable conviction?

We can bring this issue into sharper relief by characterizing it as an apparent conflict between intellectual virtue and conviction, both of which, as we have noted, seem to be important to the good life of human flourishing. This is because *intellectual humility* itself seems to be an important intellectual virtue, one that is closely related to the moderate scepticism that we saw above was plausibly part of the virtuous life. Isn't the lack of intellectual humility intellectual arrogance, or dogmatism? And wouldn't someone who embraced the moderate scepticism that we set out be inclined to be intellectually humble in their opinions rather than intellectually arrogant? In particular, when faced with disagreements with apparently reasonable people, wouldn't they be willing not just to rationally engage with these people, but also to downgrade their confidence in their own opinions, at least temporarily? Indeed, one might think that intellectual humility just is a matter of having a downgraded assessment of one's intellectual abilities and achievements, such that rather than regarding oneself as knowing it all, one instead treats oneself as being a highly fallible agent with an imperfect grasp of the truth, and hence willing to learn from others around one. But on this conception of intellectual humility, what room could there possibly be for conviction in a virtuous life?

This apparent tension between intellectual humility as an intellectual virtue and conviction can be resisted, but to do so we need to understand exactly what intellectual humility as an intellectual virtue looks like. The mistake made in the foregoing is to treat such a virtue as being entirely inwards focused. What I mean by this is that the account of intellectual humility in play is all about how one assesses oneself, from an intellectual point of view.

The way we just expressed this point was that to be intellectually humble involves one effectively having an inaccurate (at least potentially anyway) conception of one's intellectual abilities and achievements, such that one regards them as less impressive than they might in fact be. That might seem initially appealing—don't humble people in general have such a downgraded conception of their abilities and achievements? On reflection, however, it ought to be clear that this can't be the right way to think about humility, intellectual or otherwise. If it were, then it would mean that having an accurate conception of one's abilities and achievements would be a vice. Applied to humility in general that's puzzling, but applied to intellectual humility in particular it's straightforwardly bizarre. Remember that the intellectual virtues are devoted to excellence in intellectual matters. If so, how could they demand inaccuracy in one's beliefs?

Taking this point on board, one might be tempted to argue instead that the point is not that one should have a downgraded assessment of one's intellectual abilities and achievements, but that one should instead embrace one's all too human intellectual failings, one's fallibility, and so forth. This is sometimes called 'owning one's intellectual limitations'. This avoids the problem of an intellectual virtue requiring inaccuracy, but it faces problems of its own, again resulting from the inwards-directed nature of the proposal. For imagine someone who is clearly intellectually superior to those around them—much smarter, much less prone to mistakes, and so on. Moreover, they are not just intellectually superior, but they also know full well that they are. If intellectual humility is just a matter of owning one's intellectual limitations, and one's intellectual limitations are so much fewer than everyone else's, then what would be wrong about such a person acting in intellectually superior ways to those around them? For example, what would be wrong with such a person discounting other peoples' viewpoints and the reasons they can offer in support of those viewpoints? It seems that on this conception of intellectual humility this kind of behaviour would be entirely compatible with one being intellectually humble.

The crux of the matter is that we need to think of intellectual humility in *outwards*-facing (or *other*-directed) terms rather than in an inwards-facing (or self-directed) way. What I mean by this is that rather than such a virtue being focused on how one regards one's own intellectual abilities and achievements it should instead be geared towards how one treats other people. In particular, what makes someone intellectually humble is the respectful way in which they intellectually engage with other people: whether they are willing to listen to alternative viewpoints, to explain the reasons they have for their own opinions, to rationally debate subject matters, and so on. The point is that while having an accurate conception of one's own intellectual abilities and achievements, and thus one's intellectual limitations, might well be something that an intellectually virtuous person would have, it is not this that grounds one's intellectual humility but rather whether one displays such intellectual respect for others.

Once we understand that this is the right way to think about intellectual humility, then the apparent conflict between acting as this intellectual virtue demands and reasonable conviction disappears. Suppose one has thought through the issues behind one's views in great detail, and is confronted with someone who has opposing views, but who has clearly not put as much thought into their own position. Being intellectually humble doesn't mean that one cannot retain one's confidence in one's opinions even when faced with this disagreement. What it does mean, however, is that one should be intellectually respectful of the other person and their opinions. One should be willing to discuss their position, explain one's own stance, and so on.

One might be suspicious of such a proposal for the following reason. If one isn't really persuaded by this opposing view, then isn't one's engagement with their position a kind of play-acting, as if one is pretending to take their position seriously when in fact one isn't? But notice that if one were play-acting in this way, then this precisely *wouldn't* be a manifestation of one's intellectual humility. Remember that intellectual virtues, like virtues more generally, are grounded in virtuous motivations. Recall that we noted above that merely acting as if one is generous—because one enjoys receiving the admiration of others, say—is not enough to manifest the virtue of generosity. It is in addition important that one's acting in a generous way is rooted in the right kinds of motivations, such as a concern for others. It follows that it is not enough to manifest the virtue of intellectual humility to act *as if* one is intellectually humble. Rather, to be intellectually humble involves behaving in ways that genuinely reflect one's intellectual concern for others, and there can be no play-acting involved in that.

That intellectual humility is compatible with reasonable conviction is crucial to the modern world we live in. We need the intellectual virtues if we are to be flourishing human beings, and as we saw embracing a moderate scepticism is part of the intellectually virtuous life. But we also need reasonable conviction. Not all points of view are rationally on a par, and that means that the intellectually virtuous should be willing to defend their opinions when necessary, and not simply capitulate in the face of such disagreement. Especially when it comes to our public life—to the defence of our political institutions, of the authority of science, and so forth—we need the virtue of intellectual courage. What is also vital, however, is that we manifest that intellectual courage in ways that are respectful of others, and that requires the virtue of intellectual humility.

If it were to turn out that intellectual virtue demanded such capitulations, then that would be a problem. Indeed, once we start capitulating in this way, then one can easily see how a moderate scepticism might collapse into the kind of radical scepticism that we saw above had such pernicious social consequences. If we are willing to downgrade our confidence in our views in this way, even though the evidence doesn't warrant this, then why should we be confident of anything we believe? The path to a radical scepticism, one that invites relativism about truth—such that we no longer care what is really true—is thus opened up.

But the choice between intellectual conviction and intellectual virtue, and the virtues of a moderate scepticism in particular, is a false one. We can have both. And that means that we can incorporate such moderate scepticism into our lives in an intellectually virtuous way without this meaning that we have to lose the strength of our convictions in the process.

Further reading and references

Chapter 1: What is scepticism?

For an introduction to the theory of knowledge that doesn't presuppose any prior knowledge of the subject, see my introductory textbook, *What is This Thing Called Knowledge?* (4th edn.) (London: Routledge, 2018). Chapters 1 and 18–20 are particularly relevant to issues covered in this chapter. See also Jennifer Nagel's *Knowledge: A Very Short Introduction* (Oxford: Oxford University Press, 2014). For an overview of the theory of knowledge that is a bit more in-depth, see my book *Epistemology* (London: Palgrave Macmillan, 2016). For a very readable introduction to the problem of scepticism, including its history, see Neil Gascoigne's book *Scepticism* (London: Acumen, 2002). See also Allan Hazlett's *A Critical Introduction to Scepticism* (London: Bloomsbury, 2014).

For a helpful introduction to some of the issues regarding truth, including the perils of adopting a relativist account of truth, see Simon Blackburn's *Truth: A Guide* (Oxford: Oxford University Press, 2007). See also Michael Lynch's *True to Life: Why Truth Matters* (Cambridge, MA: MIT Press, 2005), and Paul Boghossian's *Fear of Knowledge: Against Relativism and Constructivism* (Oxford: Oxford University Press, 2007). The reader might also find Harry Frankfurt's seminal work on 'bullshit', and what is so problematic about it, very useful in this regard. See *On Bullshit* (Princeton, NJ: Princeton University Press, 2005). For a comprehensive overview of the philosophical literature on relativism—which, the reader should note, extends well beyond the specific kind of relativism about truth that we have looked at here—see Maria Baghramian and Adam Carter's 2015 entry on 'Relativism' in the *Stanford Encyclopedia of Philosophy*, ed. E. Zalta (https://plato.stanford.edu/entries/relativism/).

For an excellent and highly engaging account of the use and abuses of science, and thereby why the scientific method is so important, see Ben Goldacre's *Bad Science* (London: Fourth Estate, 2008). For a useful discussion of our fallibility, and its epistemological ramifications, see Stephen Hetherington's entry on 'Fallibilism' in the *Internet Encyclopedia of Philosophy*, ed. J. Fieser and B. Dowden (https://www.iep.utm.edu/fallibil/). See also Baron Reed's related discussion of certainty and its relevance to epistemology in his 2008 entry on 'Certainty' for the *Stanford Encyclopedia of Philosophy*, ed. E. Zalta (https://plato.stanford.edu/entries/certainty/).

For more on the notion of an epistemic reason, and more generally how reasons are important in epistemology, see Kurt Sylvan's entry on 'Reasons in Epistemology' in *Oxford Bibliographies: Philosophy*, ed. D. H. Pritchard (DOI: 10.1093/OBO/9780195396577-0183). For an accessible treatment of how one might apply epistemology to practical questions, such as how to spot a conspiracy theory, or how to determine which 'experts' one should believe, see David Coady's *What to Believe Now: Applying Epistemology to Contemporary Issues* (Oxford: Wiley-Blackwell, 2012). See also the entries collected in David Coady and James Chase's new edited volume, *The Routledge Handbook to Applied Epistemology* (London: Routledge, 2018). Part four of my introductory epistemology textbook, *What is This Thing Called Knowledge?* (4th edn.) (London: Routledge, 2018), offers an accessible discussion of a range of topics in 'applied' epistemology, including chapters on the epistemology of education, politics, law, and technology. For an interesting, and accessible, contemporary work that blends sceptical, epistemological, and political ideas, see Michael Lynch's *In Praise of Reason* (Cambridge, MA: MIT Press, 2012).

For a classic discussion of the absurd, see Thomas Nagel's 'The Absurd', *Journal of Philosophy* 68 (1971), 716–27. For an existentialist take on the absurd, see Albert Camus's famous 1942 essay, 'The Myth of Sisyphus'. For a contemporary volume that contains a good English translation of this essay (by Justin O'Brien), see *The Myth of Sisyphus and Other Essays* (London: Vintage, 1991). For an epistemological twist on this issue, one that brings in the problem of radical scepticism, see my 'Absurdity, *Angst* and The Meaning of Life', *Monist* 93 (2010), 3–16.

Chapter 2: Is knowledge impossible?

For an accessible introduction to the problem of radical scepticism, see chapter 6 of my epistemology textbook, *Epistemology* (London: Palgrave Macmillan, 2016). For a much more detailed overview of the literature on radical scepticism, see Peter Klein's 2015 entry on 'Skepticism', in the *Stanford Encyclopedia of Philosophy*, ed. E. Zalta (https://plato.stanford.edu/entries/skepticism/). John Cottingham has a good contemporary translation of Descartes's *Meditations on First Philosophy*, published by Cambridge University Press (Cambridge, 1996). For an influential commentary on Descartes's scepticism, see Bernard Williams's *Descartes: The Project of Pure Enquiry* (London: Penguin, 1978). See also Steven Luper's article on 'Cartesian Skepticism' in the *Routledge Companion to Epistemology*, ed. S. Bernecker and D. H. Pritchard, 414–24 (London: Routledge, 2010). For a nuanced discussion of Descartes's epistemology more generally, see Stephen Gaukroger's article on 'René Descartes', also in the *Routledge Companion to Epistemology*, ed. S. Bernecker and D. H. Pritchard, 678–86 (London: Routledge, 2010). The metaphor regarding the lack of 'doctors' in New York City comes from chapter 2 of Barry Stroud's seminal *The Significance of Philosophical Scepticism* (Oxford: Oxford University Press, 1984). This is a book that is well worth reading for a sympathetic, historically-informed, and highly influential, account of Cartesian scepticism. For a comprehensive historical anthology of writings on scepticism, see Richard Popkin and J. R. Maia Neto's edited volume, *Skepticism: An Anthology* (Amherst, MA: Prometheus Books, 2007). For a contemporary anthology of sceptical writings, including useful commentaries, see Keith DeRose and Ted Warfield's *Skepticism: A Contemporary Reader* (Oxford: Oxford University Press, 1999). For an excellent recent collection of articles on scepticism, including its history, see Diego Machuca and Baron Reed's edited volume, *Skepticism: From Antiquity to the Present* (London: Bloomsbury, 2018).

For an in-depth account of the structure of sceptical arguments, see part one of my recent monograph devoted to radical scepticism, *Epistemic Angst: Radical Skepticism and the Groundlessness of Our Believing* (Princeton, NJ: Princeton University Press, 2015). To learn more about the closure principle, see Steven Luper's 2016 entry on 'Epistemic Closure' in the *Stanford Encyclopedia of Philosophy*, ed. E. Zalta (https://plato.stanford.edu/entries/closure-epistemic/). See also John Collins's entry on 'Epistemic Closure Principles' in the *Internet Encyclopedia of Philosophy*, ed. J. Fieser and B. Dowden (https://www.iep.utm.edu/epis-clo/). The idea that there is something incoherent in denying an instance of closure—what he refers to as uttering an 'abominable conjunction'—can be found in Keith DeRose's article, 'Solving the Skeptical Problem', *Philosophical Review* 104 (1995), 1–52.

If you want to read more about philosophical paradoxes, then a great place to start would be Mark Sainsbury's book, *Paradoxes* (3rd edn.) (Cambridge: Cambridge University Press, 2009). For an entertaining collection of philosophical discussions of the film *The Matrix*, which is probably the closest Hollywood has got to presenting a BIV-style radical sceptical scenario, see Christopher Grau's *Philosophers Explore the Matrix* (Oxford: Oxford University Press, 2005). For more about sceptical themes in mainstream cinema, see Philipp Schmerheim's book, *Skepticism Films: Knowing and Doubting the World in Contemporary Cinema* (London: Bloomsbury, 2015). For a more demanding, though nonetheless brilliant, book in the same vein, see Stanley Cavell's *Disowning Knowledge: In Seven Plays of Shakespeare* (2nd edn.) (Cambridge: Cambridge University Press, 2003), which is a fascinating discussion of sceptical motifs in Shakespeare's plays.

Chapter 3: Defending knowledge

The two main papers where G. E. Moore advances his response to radical scepticism are 'A Defence of Common Sense', *Contemporary British Philosophy* (2nd series), ed. J. H. Muirhead (London: Allen & Unwin, 1925), and 'Proof of an External World', *Proceedings of the British Academy* 25 (1939), 273–300. Note that the sceptical problem that Moore is dealing with is rather different to how we are formulating it here (e.g. he never discusses BIVs or the closure principle). Indeed, Moore's concerns aren't always specifically about radical scepticism at all, as he was also interested in arguing against a closely related view known as *idealism*. This is the idea that the external world, as we have characterized it anyway, doesn't exist. The arguments for idealism and external world scepticism are often very similar, but it is important to appreciate that they are distinct theses. The external world sceptic isn't saying that the external world doesn't exist, after all, but only that you can't know anything about it. For more about idealism, see the excellent 2015 survey article on 'Idealism' by Paul Guyer and Rolf-Peter Horstmann in the *Stanford Encyclopedia of Philosophy*, ed. E. Zalta (https://plato.stanford.edu/entries/idealism/). For a general discussion of Moore's commonsense approach to scepticism, see Noah Lemos's article 'Moore and Skepticism', in the *Oxford Handbook of Skepticism*, ed. J. Greco, 330–47 (Oxford: Oxford University Press, 2008). For a defence of the commonsense approach more generally in philosophy, including as it appears in the work of Thomas Reid, see Lemos's book, *Common Sense: A Contemporary Defense* (Cambridge: Cambridge University Press, 2004). For more on Reid's epistemology in particular, see Ryan Nichols' article, 'Thomas Reid', in the *Routledge Companion to Epistemology*, ed. S. Bernecker and D. H. Pritchard, 717–29 (London: Routledge, 2010). If you're interested in a way of thinking about our everyday knowledge such that we might well know the denials of radical sceptical hypotheses (in a broadly Moorean spirit), see my recent monograph, *Epistemological Disjunctivism* (Oxford: Oxford University Press, 2012). This book in turn develops a proposal made by John McDowell—see, for example, his paper, 'Knowledge and the Internal', *Philosophy and Phenomenological Research* 55 (1995), 877–93. For a very different (but still broadly Moorean) defence of our knowledge of the denials of radical sceptical hypotheses, see John Greco's book, *Putting Skeptics in Their Place: The Nature of Skeptical Arguments and Their Role in Philosophical Inquiry* (Cambridge: Cambridge University Press, 2000).

For some of the key defences of a contextualist response to radical scepticism, see Keith DeRose's 'Solving the Skeptical Problem', *Philosophical Review* 104 (1995), 1–52, David Lewis's 'Elusive Knowledge', *Australasian Journal of Philosophy* 74 (1996), 549–67, and Stewart Cohen's 'Contextualism and Skepticism', *Philosophical Issues* 10 (2000), 94–107. There is also a very interesting version of contextualism presented by Ram Neta that shifts the focus from knowledge to evidence. See his articles, 'S Knows that P', *Noûs* 36 (2002), 663–89, and 'Contextualism and the Problem of the External World', *Philosophy and Phenomenological Research* 66 (2003), 1–31. For an overview of recent work on contextualism and scepticism, see Patrick Rysiew's article on 'Contextualism' in the *Routledge Companion to Epistemology*, ed. S. Bernecker and D. H. Pritchard, 523–35 (London: Routledge, 2010). If you want to know more about the philosophical issues raised by indexicals (which extend far beyond their possible import for contextualism), see David Braun's 2015 entry on 'Indexicals' in the *Stanford Encyclopedia of Philosophy*, ed. E. Zalta (https://plato.stanford.edu/entries/indexicals/).

The notebooks that make up Wittgenstein's *On Certainty* were published in 1969, ed. G. E. M. Anscombe and G. H. von Wright, trans. D. Paul and G. E. M. Anscombe (Oxford: Blackwell). The quotations offered in this chapter are both from this translation (§§341–3 and §125, respectively). As with Moore, note that Wittgenstein's characterization of the sceptical problem is somewhat different to how we have characterized it, especially in terms of how there is no mention of BIVs or the closure principle. Note too that since these are notebooks which Wittgenstein never edited himself or intended for publication, it follows that they are open to a wide range of interpretations. The interpretation of Wittgenstein that I offer here is my own—for more details, see especially part two of my *Epistemic Angst: Radical Skepticism and the Groundlessness of Our Believing* (Princeton, NJ: Princeton University Press, 2015). Note that I further claim in this work that my interpretation of Wittgenstein has the resources to preserve the closure principle while still evading the radical sceptical puzzle. There is a wealth of literature on Wittgenstein's line on scepticism in *On Certainty*. For some key discussions in this regard, see Marie McGinn's *Sense and Certainty: A Dissolution of Scepticism* (Oxford: Blackwell, 1989), Michael Williams's *Unnatural Doubts: Epistemological Realism and the Basis of Scepticism* (Oxford: Blackwell, 1991), Daniele Moyal-Sharrock's *Understanding Wittgenstein's On Certainty* (London: Palgrave Macmillan, 2004), Annalisa Coliva's *Extended Rationality: A Hinge Epistemology* (London: Palgrave Macmillan, 2015), and Genia Schönbaumsfeld's *The Illusion of Doubt* (Oxford: Oxford University Press, 2016).

See also Coliva's *Moore and Wittgenstein: Scepticism, Certainty, and Common Sense* (London: Palgrave Macmillan, 2010), which specifically contrasts Moorean and Wittgensteinian responses to radical scepticism. For a survey of recent work on Wittgensteinian epistemology, and his associated response to radical scepticism, see my article, 'Wittgenstein on Hinge Commitments and Radical Scepticism in *On Certainty*', in the *Blackwell Companion to Wittgenstein*, ed. H.-J. Glock and J. Hyman, 563–75 (Oxford: Blackwell, 2017).

For two influential rationales for denying the closure principle—albeit very different to the Wittgensteinian rationale described here—see Fred Dretske's article, 'Epistemic Operators', *Journal of Philosophy* 67 (1970), 1007–23, and part 3 of Robert Nozick's book, *Philosophical Explanations* (Oxford: Oxford University Press, 1981). For critical discussion of this way of denying the closure principle, there is an informative exchange between Dretske and John Hawthorne in part 2 of *Contemporary Debates in Epistemology*, ed. E. Sosa and M. Steup, 13–46 (Oxford: Blackwell, 2005). This features Dretske making the case against closure, Hawthorne making the case for, and Dretske responding to Hawthorne.

Chapter 4: Scepticism as a way of life

The main work where Aristotle develops his ethical views, and thereby discusses the virtues (including the intellectual virtues), is the *Nicomachean Ethics*. There is an excellent contemporary edition of this work by Terence Irwin (2nd edn., Indianapolis, IN: Hackett, 1999). For an overview of Aristotle's ethics, see Richard Kraut's 2018 entry on this topic in the *Stanford Encyclopedia of Philosophy*, ed. E. Zalta (https://plato.stanford.edu/entries/aristotle-ethics/). For an important contemporary ethical work that incorporates the ancient idea of ethical concerns as being much broader than morality, see Bernard Williams's book, *Ethics and the Limits of Philosophy* (Cambridge, MA: Harvard University Press, 1985). For an overview of Aristotle's epistemology, see Richard Patterson's article on 'Aristotle', in the *Routledge Companion to Epistemology*, ed. S. Bernecker and D. H. Pritchard, 666–77 (London: Routledge, 2010). For a key contemporary defence of an Aristotelian account of the intellectual virtues, see Linda Zagzebski's important book, *Virtues of the Mind: An Inquiry into the Nature of Virtue and the Ethical Foundations of Knowledge* (Cambridge: Cambridge University Press, 1995). For some other recent influential defences of the role of the virtues in knowledge, see Ernest Sosa's books, *A Virtue Epistemology: Apt Belief and Reflective Knowledge* (Oxford: Oxford University Press, 2007), and *Reflective Knowledge: Apt Belief and Reflective Knowledge* (Oxford: Oxford University Press, 2009), and John Greco's *Achieving Knowledge: A Virtue-Theoretic Account of Epistemic Normativity* (Cambridge: Cambridge University Press, 2010). For a helpful overview of virtue epistemology, see Jonathan Kvanvig's article on 'Virtue Epistemology' in the *Routledge Companion to Epistemology*, ed. S. Bernecker and D. H. Pritchard, 199–207 (London: Routledge, 2010). For a useful survey of work on the intellectual virtues in particular, see Heather Battaly's article, 'Intellectual Virtues', in the *Handbook of Virtue Ethics*, ed. S. van Hooft, 177–87 (London: Acumen, 2014). For a systematic recent account of the intellectual virtues, see Jason Baehr's *The Inquiring Mind: On Intellectual Virtues and Virtue Epistemology* (Oxford: Oxford University Press, 2011). For a contemporary discussion of the role of intellectual vice in political settings, see Quassim Cassam's book, *Vices of the Mind: From the Intellectual to the Political* (Oxford: Oxford University Press, 2019).

For a contemporary edition of Sextus Empiricus's *Outlines of Pyrrhonism*, see the version edited by R. G. Bury (Amherst, MA: Prometheus Books, 1990). For more information about Sextus Empiricus, see Benjamin Morison's 2014 entry on 'Sextus Empiricus' in the *Stanford Encyclopedia of Philosophy*, ed. E. Zalta (https://plato.stanford.edu/entries/sextus-empiricus/). For a helpful overview of Pyrrhonian scepticism, see Richard Bett's article on this topic in the *Routledge Companion to Epistemology*, ed. S. Bernecker and D. H. Pritchard, chapter 37 (London: Routledge, 2010). For a recent defence of the idea that Pyrrhonism should be construed as a certain kind of open-ended inquiry, see Casey Perin's book, *The Demands of Reason: An Essay on Pyrrhonian Scepticism* (Oxford: Oxford University Press, 2012). For further discussion of the (exegetically contentious) question of how to understand the focus of Pyrrhonian scepticism, and in particular to what extent it excludes everyday beliefs, see

Myles Burnyeat, 'Can the Skeptic Live his Skepticism?', in *Doubt and Dogmatism: Studies in Hellenistic Epistemology*, ed. J. Barnes, M. Burnyeat, and M. Schofield, chapter 3 (Oxford: Clarendon Press, 1980), Jonathan Barnes, 'The Beliefs of a Pyrrhonist', *Proceedings of the Cambridge Philological Society* 208 (1982), 1–29, and Michael Frede, 'The Sceptic's Two Kinds of Assent and the Question of the Possibility of Knowledge', in *Philosophy in History: Essays on the Historiography of Philosophy*, ed. R. Rorty, J. B. Schneewind, and Q. Skinner, chapter 11 (Cambridge: Cambridge University Press, 1984). To find out more about Pyrrho of Elis, see Richard Bett's 2018 entry on 'Pyrrho' in the *Stanford Encyclopedia of Philosophy*, ed. E. Zalta (https://plato.stanford. edu/entries/pyrrho/). To learn more about the connections between Pyrrhonian sceptical practices and Madhyamaka Buddhism, see Christopher Beckwith's book, *Greek Buddha: Pyrrho's Encounter with Early Buddhism in Central Asia* (Princeton: Princeton University Press, 2015), and Robin Brons's article, 'Life Without Belief: A Madhyamaka Defence of the Liveability of Pyrrhonism', *Philosophy East and West* 68 (2018), 329–51. If you want to find out more about Madhyamaka Buddhism itself, see Dan Arnold's entry on 'Madhyamaka Buddhist Philosophy' in the *Internet Encyclopedia of Philosophy*, ed. J. Fieser and B. Dowden (https://www.iep.utm.edu/b-madhya/).

For the classic historical account of the role of scepticism in the scientific revolution, see Richard Popkin's magisterial, and highly influential, *The History of Scepticism: From Savonarola to Bayle* (Oxford: Oxford University Press, 2003). To understand the distinctive motivations of the ancient Greek philosophers, one can do no better than consult the highly readable account offered by Pierre Hadot in his book, *What is Ancient Philosophy?*, trans. M. Chase (Cambridge, MA: Belknap Press, 2002). For a useful recent discussion of Agrippa's Trilemma, see Michael Williams's article, 'The Agrippan Problem, Then and Now', *International Journal for the Study of Skepticism* 5 (2005), 80–106.

For a recent overview of work on the epistemology of disagreement, see Bryan Frances and Jonathan Matheson's 2018 entry on 'Disagreement' in the *Stanford Encyclopedia of Philosophy*, ed. E. Zalta (https://plato.stanford.edu/entries/disagreement/). The idea that disagreement with our epistemic peers requires us to lower our confidence in our beliefs is very common in the literature. For some influential versions of this proposal, see David Christensen's 'Epistemology of Disagreement: The Good News', *Philosophical Review* 116 (2007), 187–217, Adam Elga's 'Reflection and Disagreement', *Noûs* 41 (2007), 478–502, and Richard Feldman's 'Reasonable Religious Disagreements', in *Philosophers Without Gods*, ed. L. Antony, 194–214 (Oxford: Oxford University Press, 2007).

For a helpful recent overview of the literature on intellectual humility, see Nancy Snow's article on this topic in the *Routledge Handbook of Virtue Epistemology*, ed. H. Battaly, chapter 15 (London: Routledge, 2018). For an influential account of modesty, which is a cognitive trait closely related to humility, as involving a downgraded assessment of one's abilities and achievements, see Julia Driver's paper, 'The Virtues of Ignorance', *Journal of Philosophy* 86 (1989), 373–84. For the key defence of the 'owning your limitations' view of intellectual humility, see Daniel Whitcomb, Heather Battaly, Jason Baehr, and Daniel Howard-Synder's article, 'Intellectual Humility: Owning our Limitations', *Philosophy and Phenomenological Research* 94 (2017), 509–39. For a defence of a version of the kind of 'outward-facing' account of intellectual humility offered here, see Robert Roberts and W. Jay Wood's book, *Intellectual Virtues: An Essay in Regulative Epistemology* (Oxford: Oxford University Press, 2007). For related proposals, see also Alessandra Tanesini's 'Intellectual Humility as Attitude', *Philosophy and Phenomenological Research* (2016, Online First, DOI: 10.1111/phpr.12326), and Maura Priest, 'Intellectual Humility: An Interpersonal Theory', *Ergo* 4.16 (2017, DOI: http://dx.doi.org/10.3998/ergo.12405314.0004.016). For further discussion of how this account of intellectual humility can be compatible with reasonable conviction, such that we don't have to automatically lower our confidence in our beliefs in the face of a disagreement with an epistemic peer, see my 'Intellectual Humility and the Epistemology of Disagreement', *Synthese* (2018, DOI: https://doi.org/10.1007/s11229-018-02024-5).

Index

A

ability knowledge 13
absurdity of existence 20–2
Academic scepticism 87
Agrippa's Trilemma 86–7
Alexander the Great 85
anti-sceptics 63–4, 71
arational convictions 61
Aristotle 79–84, 88
art, relativism 10
astrology 1–2
ataraxia 85–6

B

belief
  vs. doubt 1–2
  epistemic reasons 15–20, 24,
    42–3
  false 27
  vs. knowledge 12–15
  rational support 61–71
brains in a vat (BIVs) 29–35,
  39–40, 51, 60
Buddhism 85

C

Cartesian scepticism 24–9

certainty 14–15, 73
  rational evaluations 64–71
circular reasoning 86–7
climate change 2–3, 5
closure principle 37–43, 45–6,
  50–3, 58–9, 70–1
cogito ergo sum (Descartes)
  25–6, 29
commonsense
  arational 61
  vs. radical scepticism 48–55,
    63–4, 66–7
conscientiousness 82–4
conspiracy theories 5, 75–6
contextualism 55–61
conviction 88–96
counterarguments 91–2
courage
  vs. cowardice 80–1
  intellectual 82, 95–6
cowardice vs. courage 80–1

D

deceptive experiences 28
Descartes, René 24–9,
  63–4
disagreements 91–3, 95
dogmatism 73–4, 83–4, 87,
  89, 91–3

doubt
    absence of epistemic reasons to
        believe 17–18
    vs. belief 1–2
    in everything 19–22
    induced by modes 85–7
    localized vs. generalized 3–4, 6
    in science 9
dreams, as radical sceptical
    hypotheses 26–8, 32–3

E

entailment propositions 37–42,
    50–1
epistemic reasons for beliefs 15–20,
    24, 42–3
epistemology 50
epoche 87
error-possibilities 19, 26–9, 35–7,
    45–6, 49–50
    ruling out 62–3
ethics 80, 82
eudaimonia 79–80, 83
everyday claims 39–43, 50–3,
    58, 67
evil demon error-possibility 28–9
existence
    indubitable 25–6
    of God 26
    meaning 20–2, 83
external world scepticism 24–9

F

faith 67–8
    vs. science 75
fallibility 73
    intellectual 93–4
    of judgements 9–12, 19
    of knowledge 36–7
    of the senses 14–15, 28
false beliefs 27
false facts 4–5

false knowledge 13–14
foundationalism 25–6, 63–4

G

generalized sceptical doubt 3–4, 6
    see also radical scepticism
God, existence 26
golden mean 80–4
good life 80–3, 88
    conviction 88–96
guesswork 16–17
gullibility 1–2, 12–13, 16–17, 19

H

hallucinations 14
hands, possession of 51–3, 66–7
'healthy' scepticism 1–2
hinge certainties 65–71
horoscopes 1–2
humility, intellectual 82, 92–6

I

Inception (film) 32–3
indexicals, context-sensitivity 56–7
infinite regress 86–7
intellectual humility 82, 92–6
intellectual limitations 93–4
intellectual tranquillity (*ataraxia*)
    85–6
intellectual virtues 82–4, 92–6

J

judgements, fallibility 9–12, 19
justice 5

K

knowledge 12–19
    context-sensitivity 55–61
    fallibility 36–7

of nothing 19–22
revisionary account 55
ruling out
error-possibilities 62–3

L

life of flourishing *see* good life
localized sceptical doubt 3–4, 6,
23, 74

M

Madhyamaka Buddhism 85
Matrix, The (film) 30
meaningful life 83
meaningless existence 20–2
Meditations on First Philosophy
(Descartes) 24–7
moderate scepticism 72–4
and virtues 83–4, 92–3
modes 85–7
Moore, G. E. 48–9, 51–5, 61, 63–4,
66–7
morality 80, 82, 88

N

Nāgārjuna 85

O

Obama, President Barack 4
objective truth 77–8
On Certainty (Wittgenstein) 61,
64–5
open-mindedness 82–4
Outlines of Pyrrhonism
(Sextus Empiricus) 85

P

perceptual knowledge 14
political views 8–9

Popova, Lyubov 10
post-truth politics 4–5
predictions 1–2, 11–12
propositional knowledge 13
propositions, closure principle
37–42, 50–1
prudential reasons for beliefs
15–16, 24
public life
conviction 90
radical scepticism in 4–5, 74–9
Pyrrho of Elis 85
Pyrrhonian scepticism 84–8

R

radical sceptical hypotheses 26–34,
36–7, 43, 66–7, 74
impossible to rule out 34–6
radical scepticism 2–5, 18, 20,
22–4
Cartesian 24–9, 32–3
and the closure principle 37–43,
45–6, 50–3, 58–9
vs. commonsense 48–55, 63–4,
66–7
contextualist response 55–61
fake experiences 29–37
vs. hinge certainty 65–71
justifications for 72–3, 78
paradox 43–6, 48–55, 58, 78
in public life 4–5, 74–9
about science 75–7
vs. virtues 83–4 *see also* brains
in a vat (BIVs)
rational evaluations 61–71
reasonable conviction 91
Reid, Thomas 48–9
relativism
and art 10
context-sensitivity 56–7, 59
justifications for 72–3
in public life 77–9
about truth 5–12, 18

Renaissance 74
revisionary account of
    knowledge 55

S

science
    vs. faith 75
    fallibility 9–12, 19
    moderate scepticism 73–4
    radical scepticism 75–7
    scepticism about 2–4
senses
    fake experiences 29–37
    fallibility 14–15, 28
Sextus Empiricus 85, 87
Sisyphus 20–1
skills vs. virtues 81–2
subjective opinion 5–12, 18

T

Truman Show, The (film) 33
Trump, Donald 4

truth
    effect of radical scepticism 4–5
    knowledge about 12–19
    objective 77–8
    relativism 5–12, 18

U

used-car salespeople 1–4

V

vices 80–1
virtues 79–82
    intellectual 82–4, 92–6

W

Wittgenstein, Ludwig 61,
    64–71

Z

Zhuang Zhou 27

AGNOSTICISM
A Very Short Introduction
Robin Le Poidevin

What is agnosticism? Is it just the 'don't know' position on God, or is there more to it than this? Is it a belief, or merely the absence of belief? Who were the first to call themselves 'agnostics'? These are just some of the questions that Robin Le Poidevin considers in this *Very Short Introduction*. He sets the philosophical case for agnosticism and explores it as a historical and cultural phenomenon. What emerges is a much more sophisticated, and much more interesting, attitude than a simple failure to either commit to, or reject, religious belief. Le Poidevin challenges some preconceptions and assumptions among both believers and non-atheists, and invites the reader to rethink their own position on the issues.

www.oup.com/vsi

BEAUTY
A Very Short Introduction
Roger Scruton

In this *Very Short Introduction* the renowned philosopher Roger
Scruton explores the concept of beauty, asking what makes an
object - either in art, in nature, or the human form - beautiful,
and examining how we can compare differing judgements of
beauty when it is evident all around us that our tastes vary so
widely. Is there a right judgement to be made about beauty?
Is it right to say there is more beauty in a classical temple than
a concrete office block, more in a Rembrandt than in last year's
Turner Prize winner? Forthright and thought-provoking, and as
accessible as it is intellectually rigorous, this introduction to the
philosophy of beauty draws conclusions that some may find
controversial, but, as Scruton shows, help us to find greater
sense of meaning in the beautiful objects that fill our lives.

A fascinating book, which I heartily recommend.

Brya Wilson, Readers Digest

CHAOS
A Very Short Introduction
Leonard Smith

Our growing understanding of Chaos Theory is having
fascinating applications in the real world - from technology to
global warming, politics, human behaviour, and even gambling
on the stock market. Leonard Smith shows that we all have an
intuitive understanding of chaotic systems. He uses accessible
maths and physics (replacing complex equations with simple
examples like pendulums, railway lines, and tossing coins) to
explain the theory, and points to numerous examples in
philosophy and literature (Edgar Allen Poe, Chang-Tzu, Arthur
Conan Doyle) that illuminate the problems. The beauty of fractal
patterns and their relation to chaos, as well as the history of
chaos, and its uses in the real world and implications for the
philosophy of science are all discussed in this *Very Short
Introduction*.

> '...Chaos...will give you the clearest (but not too painful idea) of
> the maths involved... There's a lot packed into this little book, and
> for such a technical exploration it's surprisingly readable and
> enjoyable - I really wanted to keep turning the pages. Smith also
> has some excellent words of wisdom about common
> misunderstandings of chaos theory...'

popularscience.co.uk

www.oup.com/vsi

EXISTENTIALISM
A Very Short Introduction
Thomas Flynn

Existentialism was one of the leading philosophical movements of
the twentieth century. Focusing on its seven leading figures,
Sartre, Nietzsche, Heidegger, Kierkegaard, de Beauvoir,
Merleau-Ponty and Camus, this *Very Short Introduction* provides
a clear account of the key themes of the movement which
emphasized individuality, free will, and personal responsibility
in the modern world. Drawing in the movement's varied
relationships with the arts, humanism, and politics, this book
clarifies the philosophy and original meaning of 'existentialism' -
which has tended to be obscured by misappropriation. Placing
it in its historical context, Thomas Flynn also highlights how
existentialism is still relevant to us today.

www.oup.com/vsi

GAME THEORY
A Very Short Introduction
Ken Binmore

Games are played everywhere: from economics to evolutionary biology, and from social interactions to online auctions. Game theory is about how to play such games in a rational way, and how to maximize their outcomes. Game theory has seen spectacular successes in evolutionary biology and economics, and is beginning to revolutionize other disciplines from psychology to political science. This *Very Short Introduction* shows how game theory can be understood without mathematical equations, and reveals that everything from how to play poker optimally to the sex ratio among bees can be understood by anyone willing to think seriously about the problem.

LAW
A Very Short Introduction
Raymond Wacks

Law underlies our society - it protects our rights, imposes
duties on each of us, and establishes a framework for the
conduct of almost every social, political, and economic activity.
The punishment of crime, compensation of the injured, and the
enforcement of contracts are merely some of the tasks of a
modern legal system. It also strives to achieve justice, promote
freedom, and protect our security. This *Very Short Introduction*
provides a clear, jargon-free account of modern legal systems,
explaining how the law works both in the Western tradition and
around the world.

www.oup.com/vsi